THE SIEGE OF BERLIN

THE SIEGE OF BERLIN

Mark Arnold-Forster

COLLINS
St James's Place, London
1979

William Collins Sons & Co. Ltd
London · Glasgow · Sydney · Auckland
Toronto · Johannesburg

First published 1979
© Mark Arnold-Forster 1979
ISBN 0 00 216739 5
Set in Monotype Imprint
Made and Printed in Great Britain by
William Collins Sons & Co. Ltd Glasgow

Acknowledgments

In writing this book I have become indebted to a distinguished host of friends and advisers. Although I was myself in Berlin during most of that city's post-war crises, no reporter can pretend to know everything that happens or even – sometimes – anything that happens.

I became indebted (in chronological order) to Group Captain Haslam and Mr P. R. Wood of the Air Historical Branch of the Ministry of Defence, London; to Squadron Leader (formerly Flying Officer) Weller; to the archivists of the Ullstein Archiv, Berlin; to the staff of Infoplan in Berlin and London; to Major Baynes of the British Army Air Corps; to the staff of the Landesarchiv, Berlin; to the staff of RIAS; to M. Phillipe Trigault of the French Military Mission in Berlin; to Dr Ulrich Biel of the Berlin Senate; to Herr Rainer Wagner; to Major John Ellis of the British Military Mission in Berlin; to my old and valued friend Friedrich Luft; to Mrs Chaim and many others at the Scherneberger Rathaus; to the careful librarians of the Berlin Huguenot Church; to Corporal (now Major) Moore; and to Air Vice Marshal Cornish, RAAF.

I would like also to emphasize my gratitude to present and former colleagues. To the prophet of reconciliation between Germans and Anglo-Saxons, Herbert Sulzbach, of the German Embassy in London. To Terence Prittie with whom I shared, as a junior partner, the coverage of Berlin isolated. To Jonathan Steele, whose book on the German Democratic Republic is a seminal work. And to my wise friend Leo Muray of the *Liverpool Daily Post* whose contributions to the state of public knowledge have often been sensational but never wrong. The *Guardian*, for the second time, has allowed me to exploit its sabbatical system and to quote from what I had written for the paper. The *Observer* also has allowed me to quote. I am grateful to both editors.

I also owe important debts to Mr Cheeseborough and Mr Dick Groom of the historical section of the British Foreign Office. In the United States I give thanks to Gail Halvorsen, formerly Lieutenant and now a retired Colonel; to Jim Huston, formerly a Captain and now a retired Colonel; to General Tunner and to General Wedemeyer, whose testimony is crucial to any proper understanding of the Berlin airlift. But I must also thank particularly Major General John Huston of the Air History Division of the US Defense Department and his staff. Their ability to produce persons and papers – as the saying goes – is unexampled. Last but by no possible means least, Mr Philip Ziegler and Miss Alison Wade of Collins. I do not understand how anyone can write a book without their help.

Contents

Illustrations and Map

With the exception of those otherwise mentioned above, all photographs are reproduced by permission of Landesbildstelle, Berlin (by courtesy of Infoplan)

Preface

West Berlin is a pleasant city of rather more than two million inhabitants who live the lives of reluctant lighthouse-keepers. They can do anything they like except freely leave their island. They are self-governing but within limits. They can dismiss the mayor, revolutionize the housing programme, encourage the arts to blossom, but they cannot go for walks in the country.

Nor can they conduct their own foreign policy or do anything on their own initiative to change their insular unnatural status. Since 3 June 1972, after a long and arduous diplomatic wrangle West Berlin became a protectorate whose status is guaranteed by the Soviet Union, the United States, Britain and France – the four Allied powers which won the war against Hitler in 1945. West Berlin's integrity, and the West Berliners' liberty are guaranteed by these four mighty powers in the same way that the integrity and liberty of Gibraltar is guaranteed by Britain. This state of affairs does not satisfy the West Berliners' main ambition which is to become a part of the West German Federal Republic with whose inhabitants they share a faith in democracy and a measure of prosperity. But their protected status, guaranteed by an international treaty, is at least more stable than and therefore preferable to the conditions under which they lived between the end of World War II in 1945 and the conclusion of the Berlin Agreement in 1972. For those twenty-seven years the West Berliners were hostages held by the Russians. Their communications with Western Europe were always at risk and could be interrupted at the whim of a Soviet General. They were surrounded, and still are, by the East German Democratic Republic which has always been a dictatorship, even though tyranny has now mellowed into autocracy.

The people who inhabit West Berlin today are the innocent victims of the quarrels between the powers whose armies defeated

Hitler in 1945 – quarrels which broke out within two years of victory and became increasingly bitter. But before the quarrels became apparent the seeds of discord over Berlin were sown at three inter-Allied conferences at Teheran, at Yalta in the Crimea and at Potsdam, which was the country seat of the Prussian kings and is to Berlin what Windsor is to London.

The decisive figures at the first two conferences were Stalin, Roosevelt, and Churchill. It has to be remembered in Churchill's favour and in Roosevelt's that the main purpose of the conferences at Teheran and Yalta was to accelerate the defeat of Hitler and his Germany. But besides defeating Germany, Stalin wanted to ensure that the Soviet Union would never again be attacked from the west as it had been, treacherously, by Hitler in 1941. To this end he wanted to shift Poland further westwards, so that its western frontier would lie along the rivers Oder and Neisse. He also wanted – though this was not clear at the time – to establish communist regimes in Eastern Europe which would be obedient to the Soviet Union. His fear, which was genuine and justifiable at that time, was of a resurgent Germany bent on revenge. He thought that he needed a glacis – a protective strip of territory under Russian domination – to safeguard the Soviet homeland against the threat of surprise aggression such as it had experienced in 1941.

The records of the Teheran and Yalta conferences are incomplete. It is not clear whether Churchill and Roosevelt understood all Stalin's preoccupations. In practice, however, they did not object to Stalin's plans. Churchill, as historian, was content to see the frontiers of Poland being decided – as they had so often been decided in the nineteenth century – by international statesmen instead of Poles. Roosevelt, more surprisingly, set aside for once the traditional American distaste for colonialism and imperialism and readily agreed to Stalin's plans.

What was left hopelessly and disastrously vague at Teheran and at Yalta was the precise status of the then German capital, Berlin. Probably the about-to-be victorious powers thought that Berlin did not matter very much. In fact it turned out to matter a great deal, and not only to the 2·1 million West Berliners. When the victorious Allies first fell out in 1947 their main argument was about whether to treat Germany as a vassal-state to be plundered, which was the Russian view, or whether the Germans were to be encouraged to stand on their own feet and recover through their own efforts from the economic and political state of perdition in which Hitler had left them. This fundamental disagreement between the victorious Allies was the root-cause of the siege of Berlin in 1948 and 1949 when the Russians severed all surface communication between Berlin and Western Europe. It was also the root-cause, though by then at one remove, of the satellite East German government's decision to build a wall round West Berlin: a wall designed not to keep West Berliners imprisoned but to prevent East Berliners and East Germans from escaping to the West.

The blockade made the division of Germany inevitable and with it the isolation of Berlin. When the West German Federal Republic was established on 23 May 1949 and when the East German Republic was formed on 7 October of the same year, it became clear that these were two separate countries, though inhabited by members of the same nation.

Their chosen constitutions turned out to be not unlike those of their protecting powers. The East German constitution resembles the Soviet – full of lofty expressions about liberty, democracy and civil rights, all of which are overshadowed and rendered void by sweeping reserve powers which allow the East German government to run East Germany as a police state. The West German constitution turned out to be not unlike that of the United States, which like West Germany is a federation. Whether they intended to or not, the rulers and voters of the two Germanies eventually conformed, constitutionally speaking, quite closely to the United States' and the Soviet Union's precepts.

West Berlin is the anomaly. The West Berliners' true affinity is with the West Germans yet they are not allowed to be West German citizens. Nor are they necessarily subject to West German legislation. The four-power agreement of 3 June 1972 guarantees free communications between West Berlin and West Germany and says that West Berlin's ties with West Germany will be maintained and developed. But West Berlin is not recognized as part of West Germany and is not 'to be governed by it'. Eager though they are to become West German citizens, the West Berliners must, perforce, continue to lead the lives of lighthouse-keepers. Their city lies east of the Iron Curtain – by about 200 miles – and the Soviet Union, partly for Stalin's original reason of defence, partly for fear of infection by democracy, will not tolerate a West German outpost within the Russian sphere of influence.

The West Berliners have endured this unwanted isolation cheerfully, resourcefully, and with a pungent sense of humour which is all their own. They have been mightily sustained at various times by outsiders of conspicuous stature and fortitude. But all the efforts of outsiders would have been in vain but for the fortitude of the West Berliners themselves. The story of West Berlin is above all the story of the courage of two million tough, unassuming, and cheerful people.

PART I

I

The Russians Take Berlin

At about midday on 2 May 1945 Captain N. I. Kruchinin and his men of the 79th Russian Guards Division extinguished resistance from a small group of soldiers who were holding out in one of three air-raid shelters in the Tiergarten, the large and leafy park in central Berlin to which the German Army had retreated in a last despairing stand against the advance of the Russians. It was the end of the Third Reich. Although the war lingered on in other parts of Germany for six more days the capture of Berlin by the Russians was the effective end of World War II.

The political importance of Berlin was acknowledged on all sides. It had been the capital of Prussia for centuries, the capital of Germany since 18 January 1871 when William I of Prussia was proclaimed German Emperor. Although Churchill, Stalin and Roosevelt had agreed earlier in 1945 at Yalta that Germany, though divided into three zones of occupation – British, American and Russian (the French zone was later carved out of the American) – should be governed by an Allied Control Council from Berlin which was to be within the Soviet zone of occupation, the Western Allies, and Churchill in particular, were much tempted to try to reach Berlin before the Russians did. The question that the politicians pondered was whether the Western powers should make an all-out effort to take Berlin themselves or accept the military reality, which was that the Russians were going to capture Berlin quite soon anyway.

By the last week of March the British and the Americans had surrounded the Ruhr while the Russians were about thirty-five miles east of Berlin. By now the Western Allies – which meant, in effect, the British and the Americans — were achieving very long daily marches in pursuit of a retreating enemy. In political circles the argument was that the capture of central Germany which the Western Allies had already achieved, might be less important, from the point of view of prestige, than the capture of Berlin. Churchill said that, if the Russians got to Berlin first, they might see themselves as having been the 'overwhelming contributor to our common victory' and that this might generate future political difficulties. But the facts spoke against him. The Russians had lost twenty million dead and had contributed overwhelmingly to the Allied victory over Germany. Anyway, whoever got to Berlin first, the Russians or the Americans, the Russians were going to hold their Western Allies to the Yalta bargain.

The Western Allied governments left the decision to their Commander-in-Chief, General Eisenhower. As a soldier, Eisenhower's reply was that he did not propose to risk the lives of his men, simply in order to gain a political advantage over an ally. Eisenhower told Washington:

> I regard it as militarily unsound at this stage [early April] of the proceedings to make Berlin a major objective, particularly in view of the fact that it is only thirty-five miles from the Russian lines. I am the first to admit that a war is waged in pursuance of political aims; and if the combined Chiefs of Staff should decide that the Allied effort to take Berlin outweighs purely military considerations in this theatre, I would cheerfully re-adjust my plans and my thinking so as to carry out such an operation.

The Combined Chiefs of Staff did not so decide. They were reluctant to override Eisenhower's military judgement which they had always respected and trusted. They were reluctant also, as any military commander would be, to ask their men to risk their lives unnecessarily in the closing stages of a war which was about to be won in any case. The most tragic death in any war is that of the last man to die on the winning side.

So the Russians arrived in Berlin first and ruled it alone for two months. They established their headquarters in Karlshorst, an eastern suburb of Berlin famous for its race-course and its trotting races. The Soviet Military Governor of Germany was Marshal Zhukov. His deputy, who was to succeed him, was Marshal Sokolovsky. Next in importance to the Soviet military administration was the chief of all Berlin policemen, Paul Markgraf, a former German officer who had been captured by the Russians and indoctrinated into the communist or Stalinist faith.

The Russians took charge of a ruined city. In capturing Berlin they did not, as has sometimes been alleged, seek to devastate the city – though considering the devastation by the Germans of Leningrad, the Russians had no special reason to spare Berlin. But the Royal Air Force and the United States Air Force had been bombing Berlin intermittently for years and, as the German air defence weakened, with increasing effect. The damage was widespread. No part of Berlin had been spared, and the Russians, surveying what they had captured, found streets impassable because of the rubble that had fallen into them from the bombed houses on either side. In wider streets the Germans had cleared a pathway between the heaps of rubble, a pathway which was usually wide enough for only two people to walk abreast.

The rubble in the streets gave rise to a new industry. This was the cleaning of bricks so that they could be used again. Many thousands of women from all over Berlin went to work to clean up the city, and to give it a chance to rebuild itself. The separation of bricks from old mortar is hard work, harsh on the hands and cold in the winter. But the army of female Berliners – the 'Trümmerfrauen', literally 'the women of the ruins' – who set their hands to cleaning bricks never faltered. Berlin has rebuilt itself now, and largely with the products of the Berliners' grandmothers' labours.

For two months the Russians had the whole of Berlin to themselves. They maintained a military government in the strictest sense. They did not really try to set up any representative German government of the city, however lowly. Instead they simply set the Berliners to work under Russian orders. They also did their best to identify and incarcerate the few leading Nazis who were still there. The Russian soldiers, who had been accustomed to living off the land ever since Hitler attacked their country in 1941, took what they needed and a good deal else besides. Berlin was the richest city they had ever captured. It contained treasures that many Russian soldiers had only heard about – wrist watches, radios, even motor cars. It was casual, not systematic plunder, but to many Berliners, that was not what it felt like.

This is not to say that the Russians neglected the administration of essential services like gas, electricity, transport and the drains. In these basic ways the Russians did their best although the problem was horrendous. What they did not do, and could not do because they were short themselves, was supply the Berliners with more than a very meagre ration of food. What they would not tolerate was the least sign of insubordination. If Paul Markgraf and his policemen could not deal with the trouble, the Russians dealt with it themselves.

The understanding at Yalta had been that Berlin would be divided into three sectors and that an Allied Kommandatura would preside over the government of the city as a whole. After the Kommandatura had been set up, with representatives of Britain, the United States, the Soviet Union, and France, the Western city commanders accused the Russians of having plundered the three Western sectors when they had had control of them. There was truth in this allegation. When the Western Allies arrived they found that some West Berlin factories were without their machines. But in this matter it is hard to blame the Russians. Their own country had been plundered. They needed the machines, as the Western Allies did not, and they imagined that the Western Allies were doing the same in the Ruhr as they were doing in Berlin.

The Russians also took firm steps to make theirs wishes known to the Germans. The *Tägliche Rundschau* (which means something akin to 'the Daily Circular') was first published by the Red Army on 15 May. It announced that the bread ration for heavy manual workers would be 600 grammes per day and that people who were not working would get 300 grammes per day. It also said, coldly, that the Red Army had captured 1,230,000 German soldiers between 9 May and 14 May as well as 101 Generals. The *Tägliche Rundschau* was, at that time, an important instrument of Russian military government in Berlin. The paper did not simply laud the Soviet victories, it also told people what to do. It was an important, though inexpensive, part of the Soviet military administration.

The fear that haunted most Berliners at that time was lest their relatives had been killed or captured on the Eastern front. In 1945 Berlin was largely a city of war-widows or of women who did not know whether they were widows or not. There was virtually no communication for many months between the Russian prisoner-of-war camps and the prisoners' relatives. The women of Berlin ached for news as they cleaned the bricks.

Meanwhile there were several meetings between the Western Allies and the Russians to settle the detailed arrangements for the Western garrisons to take up their positions in the three Western sectors of the city. Simultaneously with this occupation of West Berlin the Western powers were to withdraw from the advanced positions they had captured east of the Elbe, territory which belonged to the Soviet zone. This exchange of territory took place during the early days of July 1945. With a proper respect for anniversaries the Second Armoured Division of the US Army arrived in West Berlin punctually on 4 July and held a parade. The Americans seldom forget the festivals hallowed by their democratic ancestors.

The negotiations which had led to the exchange of territory between the Allies had shown, already, that the Russians were not prepared to do much to help the Western Allies feed and care for the population of West Berlin. Zhukov insisted that West Berlin should draw its supplies of coal from the Ruhr in the British zone of West Germany. Asked whether Berlin could not continue to draw its coal from its traditional suppliers in Silesia, Zhukov said that Silesia was now Polish territory over which he had no jurisdiction. It was the same with food. Zhukov said he had been supplying the Western sectors with food from the reserve stocks of the Red Army and could not continue to do this indefinitely. General Lucius D. Clay, deputy to General Eisenhower, and first American Military Governor, contrived generally to give the impression that he ate fire for breakfast and enjoyed the taste, but on this occasion he agreed with Zhukov: 'We could not expect the ill-nourished Russians to eat less in order to feed Berlin.'

Early in July the Western Allies took stock of what they had found in Berlin. Three fire stations out of four had been destroyed. The water mains were leaking in 3000 places. Dead bodies remained in the canals. The sewage system was badly damaged. In one western borough, Steglitz, a survey of the housing available showed that 3260 homes out of 14,000 had been destroyed, a further 3200 were uninhabitable, and in the 7500 homes which remained, 10,000 out of 43,000 rooms had been seriously damaged. In another borough, Schoeneberg, 45% of the housing had been destroyed completely, 15% had been heavily damaged and a mere 5% had been spared. These were the woeful conditions in the city for which the four victorious Allies had become jointly responsible. Had the Berliners been as woeful as their living conditions and their surroundings nothing could have been accomplished. But what the Allies were to witness over the next four years was a demonstration of unexampled resilience. The Berliners, more than most people, despise despair. Gradually they mended the drains; they cleared the rubble; they mended the water mains; in spite of appalling shortages of materials, they rehoused themselves. The government of Berlin was still an Allied matter but it was the Berliners who did the work. And as they toiled, and as the women cleaned the bricks, they began to notice that their conquerors were falling out among themselves.

2

The Conception of the West German Republic

The quarrel between the victorious Allies was about whether it would be safer and better to bleed Germany white or to forestall the revival of Nazism by insuring against a repetition of the economic chaos of the 1920s which brought Hitler to power. The Soviet Union wanted to bleed Germany white. The British and the Americans wanted Germany to prosper.

Each point of view was understandable. The Russians wanted everything they could get out of Germany because they needed it themselves and because they felt that the Germans owed it to them. They had been treacherously attacked in 1941 (treacherously because the Molotov-Ribbentrop Pact of 1939 had made them Germany's ally) and they had lost twenty million dead – the equivalent of twice the population of Pennsylvania, two and a half Londons, or forty Dresdens. Their land had been laid waste either by the Germans or because in self-defence they had scorched their own earth. These were experiences that no one could forget and which had impoverished Russia cruelly. The inhabitants of the Soviet zone could have had no cause for surprise at the Soviet reparations policy.

The Americans, whose land had not been scourged by war, were at first inclined to agree with the Russians. The so-called Morgenthau Plan, briefly endorsed by Churchill and Roosevelt at their conference in Quebec in 1944, foresaw a pastoral Germany, deprived of industry, robbed of the means for making wealth, and therefore militarily harmless. But the Americans changed their minds. By 1947 they had discarded Morgenthau. So had the British and for far-sighted reasons. The essence of the British argument has been best expounded by Brigadier P. K. Debenham of the Coldstream Guards, one of the economic advisers to the

British Military Governor. It had much in common with the arguments used, in vain, by John Maynard Keynes when he tried to prevent chaos and revolution after World War I.

> Hitler gained power in the circumstances of the financial crisis of 1929 to 1933 which convinced the Germans that the Weimar constitution was unworkable and that a higher degree of concentration of authority at the centre was necessary. There is every reason to suppose that, if we impose on Germany a financial constitution which will not work, the same consequences will follow, and that later we shall have either to accept considerable modifications under the pressure of events, or to condemn Germany to the continuation of economic disorders which may endanger law and order. Furthermore financial centralization is in effect an alternative to centralization in other fields. If we deny Germany the power to conduct her finances in an orderly manner, she will be forced to maintain in being economic and physical controls having the same ultimate purpose.

In other words, Germany must be given a strong, central financial system because the alternative was renewed financial chaos leading to another centralized regime which might be as dangerous as Hitler's.

President Truman and the British Prime Minister, Clement Attlee (who had now succeeded Churchill), were laconic men and had to consider public opinion at home; so they never actually announced that they wanted West Germany to prosper or that they wanted defeated enemies to recover as quickly as possible. This, however, was their firm joint policy. It upset the Russians, but it ought to be remembered in Truman's favour and in Attlee's.

In 1946 also there was the immediate problem that West Germany, having been conquered, was costing the Allies too much. It was costing too much because it was failing to prosper. It was failing to prosper because it was divided into three separate zones of occupation and because of inflation. The fragmentation of West Germany prevented the development of a strong economy. The demented rate at which Hitler's Reichsmark was losing its value prevented the restoration of Germany's wealth. On both counts the British and American taxpayers were losing out. And West Berlin also was a part of their burden.

Traditionally, the West Germans had imported much of their food from East Germany. With Poland occupying most of the East German grain-growing territory and with the Russians in occupation of the Soviet zone, these imports had stopped. The Russians and the Poles needed the food for themselves. In effect, the British and American governments found themselves obliged to import large quantities of grain and other food from North America in order to prevent the Germans starving. It was a heavy burden, particularly for Britain whose wealth had been used up during the war. By 1947 there were about thirty-four million inhabitants of the Western zones who needed to be fed, as well as about seven million refugees from Poland, East Germany and Czechoslovakia.

The West German economic difficulties were self-perpetuating. Because food was short, the West German industrial workers did not have the energy to work as hard as they would have wished. Because their output, along with their productivity, was low, the British and American zones were not exporting nearly enough industrial goods to pay for the imported food. Another reason for comparatively low industrial output was that the two zones were economically complementary to each other. Broadly speaking the heavy industry – the coal mines and the steel mills – was in the British zone, whereas the more sophisticated manufacturing industry was in the American zone. The British zone produced the raw materials for the industry in the American zone but, because the zones were separate, industry in the American zone was being bureaucratically starved of raw materials.

Mr Justice James F. Byrnes, the American Director of War Mobilization and Reconversion, agreed with Clay and the American political adviser Robert Murphy that a merger would benefit both Britain and America as well as the Germans who lived in their zones. The British Foreign Minister, Ernest Bevin, agreed with Byrnes. They would have liked the French to come in too, so as to make West Germany into a single economic unit which could draw some, at least, of its food supplies from the French zone which was more nearly pastoral than the other two. But the French government, still then fearful lest Germany should get too strong, refused to join. Byrnes and Bevin went ahead on their own. Their resolve was strengthened by the obvious reluctance of the Russians to allow the Soviet zone to become part of an economically united Germany. The Russians criticized with much vigour the decision to merge the two Western zones. Byrnes and Bevin were unmoved. But they decided that they must at least make a formal offer to the Russians.

On 18 July 1946 Clay delivered the offer in the Control Council:

> Since the zones of Germany are not self-supporting of themselves and since treating two zones or more as an economic unit would better this situation in the zones concerned, the United States representatives in Germany will join with the representatives of any other occupying power or powers in measures to treat their respective zones as an economic unit, pending four-power agreement to carry out the Potsdam provision regarding the treatment of all Germany as an economic unit and the reaching of a balanced economy throughout Germany . . .

The policy behind the offer had been memorably stated by US Secretary of State Marshall in the Council of Foreign Ministers on 11 July:

> The United States government does not want a peace of vengeance and it is convinced that the economic recovery of Germany along peaceful lines is necessary to the economic revival of Europe. It desires the denazification of Germany which will encourage democratic forces who otherwise may feel they cannot exert themselves with a fair chance. The sure way to encourage the growth of democratic forces in Germany is to state in definite terms the conditions of settlement, to fix German disarmament measures and the reparations which it must pay. The German people will then realize that the harder they work the sooner they will be allowed to share in

the benefits of European recovery. Germany's future boundaries should likewise be defined so that the German people may know that, as long as they adhere to the settlement, no interference will be given to their reconstruction efforts, which will help both themselves and all of Europe.

While controls and security forces must remain for a long time in Germany, mass occupation and military government continued over a long period could defeat our own purposes. The German people must have the opportunity to minimize the certain difficulties and hardships of their situation by their own efforts so that they will learn not to blame their trials on Allied occupation but rather, and properly, on the devastating war of aggression which their leaders let loose.

Marshall's statement was prophetic. The amalgamation of the British and American zones provided the economic basis for West German recovery and – because the amalgamation had to be made to work – it created a need for German institutions which would have responsibility throughout both zones. By the autumn of 1946 Clay and the British Military Governor, Sir Brian Robertson, had appointed German executive committees for economics, food and agriculture, transport, communications, the civil service, and finance. Robertson was the perfect counterpart to the firebrand Clay, a man whose imperturbability was as solid as the cliffs of Dover. They differed from each other as chalk from cheese but worked together successfully and, on the whole, harmoniously. At first, so that the Russians could not accuse them of setting up a unitary state, they scattered their executive committees far and wide. It was not the most efficient way to run a country but it was politically unobjectionable and it did provide a large part of West Germany with its first, embryonic, post-war German government. It was not very high-powered because the Allies continued to take the main decisions. But it was German.

To guide the work of the executive committees Clay and Robertson established an elected Economic Council in Frankfurt. It had fifty-two members chosen by the existing *Landtage* or State legislatures. In a modest way they constituted Germany's first freely elected government since the days of the Weimar Republic. But it was still weak in that the Allies had the overriding power: the Council and its committees advised but did not govern. Clay and Robertson recognized that the Council did not have sufficient executive powers for effective co-ordination of the German agencies. They 'proposed to continue to participate in the Allied Control Council unless it was broken up by others. We anticipated difficulty in Berlin and recommended that we stay there regardless of any Soviet pressures.' Nevertheless, even then, during the winter of 1946–7, Clay and Robertson were already looking forward to the creation of a West German Democratic State.

The next giant stride towards this end was to be the creation of a new German currency. General Clay raised it in January 1947. He said he wanted urgent consideration of a separate currency for the British and American zones.

The Russians, however, were losing patience. On 4 March 1947 the Soviet government gave vent to its feelings in one of its newspapers. *Izvestia* had got wind of General Clay's proposal. It said that the British and Americans were clearly preparing to introduce a separate currency in their zones and that the West German economy, unlike the Eastern one, was dominated by capitalists and war profiteers. 'The new monetary unit', said *Izvestia*, 'is to fulfil the function of a golden chain forcibly linking Germany with the notorious Western bloc.'

But the notorious Western bloc had real problems. In London economists were grappling as best they could, and in some degree of despair, with the chaos that was the legacy of Hitler's Reichsmark, still circulating freely throughout Germany. Export prices for German goods were as wayward as the Reichsmark itself. An enormous range of exchange rates was in force with some exports being priced at 10 Reichsmarks to the pound and others at 30 or 40. (Spare parts for Dutch tugs were exported at 10 Reichsmarks to the pound whereas machinery for making ruberoid linoleum was being exported at an exchange rate of 30·5.) The British, who tried hard and long to turn chaos into order, became irritated with the Americans who were setting different exchange rates of their own. In the American zone toys were cheap. Spare parts for Bosch electrical equipment for automobiles were expensive. The British view was that the system in force in the British zone, unsatisfactory though it was, did give German exporters an incentive to export, whereas the American system, which sought to give exporters only the internal price in Reichsmarks, did not provide incentives. Britain, in any case, had a more pressing motive than the Americans to boost German exports, for Britain had a serious balance of payments deficit. The cost of running the British occupation was heavy, largely because the British zone was a net importer of food. The sooner the Germans could export more, the better for the British.

At meetings in Berlin during March 1947 American and British officials exchanged some quite harsh words. There was a subsidiary quarrel, too, about the exchange rate for the future Deutschemark should it ever be launched. The Americans wanted it to be worth 30 American cents. The British wanted 20 cents. On the very day that *Izvestia* was nurturing dark suspicions about an Anglo-American plot, the reality was an Anglo-American quarrel.

Presently the Russians found another bone to pick. They complained of the existence of a British occupation currency, used to pay the troops. The money was called British Armed Forces Service Vouchers (BAFSVs) and was based on sterling. The Russians said that this was wrong, unfair, and divisive because it was equivalent to a second currency. The occupying powers should only deal in Reichsmarks until the final currency reform. The British replied by pointing out that the restaurant at the Russian-organized Leipzig Trade Fair would only accept US dollars, Swiss francs, Swedish kronor or sterling.

By the end of March 1947 the British and the Americans had made substantial progress – with which the Russians seem to have been at least temporarily in agreement – about what to do in order to convert Reichsmarks into the new Deutschemarks. With more than a year to go before the actual event, all four Allies agreed, more or less, that 70% of all money and bank deposits in Reichsmarks would be cancelled altogether, that 20% would remain blocked and that 10% would be payable. Ten Deutschemarks would be paid out in return for 100 Reichsmarks.

There were also detailed and agreed proposals for dealing with debts. Trading debts would be honoured fully. Mortgages would be honoured up to 50%. Other private debts would be reduced to 30% of their Reichsmark value but of this only 10% would be payable and the rest blocked.

Even so the British were still impatient. The American plan was to deal with all the problems of currency reform sequentially. They wanted to settle the printing of notes before tackling financial reform, to settle financial reform before tackling the price structure, and to settle the price structure before fixing a conversion rate for the Deutschemark. The British, on the other hand, thought it best to deal with all four problems simultaneously because to do otherwise would take too long.

The British proposals for currency reform were both far-sighted and detailed, and in the end most of them prevailed over the American proposals. They were the work of the unsung and overworked army of senior British public servants and, in particular, of Debenham and – later on – Professor Cecil Weir of Glasgow University.

Their starting point – a not unnatural one in 1947 – was that any future German financial system must contain safeguards against the repetition of the chaotic situation which helped to bring Hitler to power. Using Debenham's arguments, the British proposed a financial system that was to be sound and centralized, making a centralized political system unnecessary – a proposal in keeping with the then still embryonic suggestions for a federal constitution for post-war Germany, a constitution which would eliminate or make difficult the concentration of power in the hands of a dictator by spreading it among West Germany's eleven federal constituents or *Länder*.

The British anticipated correctly the creation of a strong and virtually independent Central Bank (the Bundesbank) which would be in charge of note-issuing policy. They foresaw the possibility that there would be large-scale unemployment in Germany, that unemployment relief would have to be financed nationally, and that the future German government should be encouraged to prepare itself from the beginning for a major effort to equalize incomes, or at least to provide benefits large enough to prevent hardship, poverty and social unrest.

The British were insistent that the main tax should be income tax because this is redistributive – it takes from the rich and offers the government the opportunity to give to the poor – and that this tax should be uniform and centrally collected by the federal government, leaving only the excise and consumption taxes (or most of them) to be collected by the *Länder*. This system, the British said, had worked well in Australia. It works well in West Germany today.

The inter-Allied quarrel over currency reform was prolonged, nasty and occasionally absurd. The first dispute in 1947 was not about economic policy at all but about the practical task of printing the new money. The Americans wanted to print it in Berlin and Leipzig (which was in the Soviet zone) simultaneously. The Americans suspected that the Russians, left to themselves in Leipzig, would simply print as many new notes as suited them, thereby replacing one case of raging inflation with another.

There was a chilly intervention by Mr Chamberlain, head of the note-printing security department at the Bank of England. He said that security at the note-printing works and the paper mills was intended to prevent fraud by employees and could not under any circumstances be a substitute for mutual confidence between the representatives of the occupying powers. If the Bank of England wanted to cheat and to issue large quantities of notes in defiance of the wishes of the other occupying powers he would not dream of using the note-printing facilities in Berlin or Leipzig. Nor could the custody of the plates make the slightest difference. He could easily produce plates from a sample of notes and then print in Britain all the extra notes he required.

'Precisely the same could be done by any of the other occupying powers. In particular, elaborate arrangements for note-printing security at Leipzig are not the slightest protection against the issue by the Soviets of large quantities of extra notes printed in the Soviet Union or elsewhere . . .' It was the Leipzig press which, Mr Chamberlain said, had produced during the war millions of counterfeit £5 notes. So perfect were they that nobody other than a mere handful of very expert note-printers could distinguish the German £5 notes from the genuine ones. 'Certainly no bank cashiers in Britain could have done so.'

Towards the end of April 1947, William H. Draper Jr, Under-Secretary of State in the Department of the Army and Clay's immediate superior in Washington, agreed that there was reason in the British case for not insisting on printing the new currency in Berlin only. Perhaps Mr Chamberlain had convinced him. Draper also agreed with Clay that the British and Americans might have to go ahead on their own with currency in their own zones, but that it would be necessary to continue discussions with the Russians until it became clear that these talks were leading nowhere.

At the end of April the *New York Times* published an accurate account of the British and American intentions, even to the extent of revealing the 70% cancellation rate for the Reichsmark. With a straight face and in chorus the British and Americans denied the report utterly.

> There is no truth in the rumours which have been circulated in London and New York to the effect that there is agreement to revalue the German mark. These rumours are untrue and mischievous. No conversion of the German currency is imminent and in fact, for technical reasons, there can be no conversion for many months.

General Clay said: 'Experienced specialists believe that at present reform would be dangerous and not advisable.'

Thus do good reporters get their come-uppance when they print news which is awkward as well as secret. Edward Morrow's story in the *New York Times* was true and so was a similar story by Norman Clark in the London *News Chronicle*. The denial, by contrast, was a bare-faced lie. But then everyone in authority tells lies about impending changes in currency rates. Even Sir Stafford Cripps, the most upright of men, did it when he had to.

In spite of Draper's conversion to the British view, the Allies were still in disagreement in October about where to print the new notes. There was also an incipient problem about the ingredients for paper. Sulphite cellulose abounded in the Soviet zone and there were plenty of rags in the American zone. The problem was to bring them together and make them into Deutschemarks.

But the time for argument was running out. Beyond the protected walls of the occupying powers' comfortable cantonments, inflation was taking hold. Journalists would buy a typewriter for a million marks. Housewives would pay 1000 marks for a dozen eggs. Farmers would barter a pig for a piano. Hyper-inflation is a plague and, like any other plague, it can demoralize a nation.

3
New Marks for Old

By the beginning of 1948 the whole of Germany and not just
Berlin was beset by the disease of inflation. The Soviet Union
was printing money in Leipzig but would not say how much. As
tortured experience in the Control Council had already shown, the
Soviet Union on the one hand and the Western Allies on the other
had contradictory ideas about how their respective parts of
Germany should develop and be governed. The British, French
and Americans foresaw a faster rate of economic growth for
Western Germany than the Soviet authorities for Eastern Germany. They also foresaw different forms of government. The
situation was intolerable. The profound, secret, three-year-old
quarrel between the Soviet, American and British governments
about Germany's future was reaching crisis point.

The first overt sign of the crisis which led to the blockade of
Berlin can be traced to the meeting of the four-power Allied
Control Council for Germany in Berlin on 20 January 1948.
Marshal Sokolovsky, by then the Soviet Military Governor for all
Germany, said for the first time formally and firmly that the
agreement between the British and the Americans to run their
two zones of occupation jointly in the interest of greater economic
efficiency constituted the setting up of a separatist German
government and was a gross violation of inter-Allied agreements.
It also violated previous agreements reached in the Control
Council itself. The French delegation reserved its position and
stood aside. The British and Americans stood their ground.

At the next meeting of the Council, on 30 January, the Allies
discussed fruitlessly the question of currency reform. On 11
February the Council decided unanimously to make a further
effort to reach joint agreement about currency within sixty days.
Clay had already been told by Washington on 9 February that:

'Our policy objective is to reach quadripartite agreement provided attainable promptly.'

On 20 March Sokolovsky brought matters to a head. He said that he suspected that what had been achieved was a bipartite agreement between Britain and America which contravened Yalta and the consequent four-power agreement reached at Potsdam. Britain and America had thus broken away from the Control Council machinery and must themselves bear the consequences. The Control Council, he said, no longer existed as an organ of government.

This was the first time that the Soviet authorities had formally questioned the continued existence of the Council in its legally constituted form. Immediately afterwards Sokolovsky, who was in the chair, adjourned the meeting. The Council, as such, never met again.

On 1 April Clay's political adviser, Robert Murphy, reported prophetically to Washington:

> . . . The charge that the Western powers have destroyed the Control Council constitutes an important element in the Soviet plan to force all three Western powers out of Berlin, in order to liquidate this remaining 'centre of reaction' east of the iron curtain. The next step may be Soviet denunciation of the agreement of 14 November [which regulated communications between West Berlin and the Western zone of Germany] and a demand for the withdrawal from Berlin of the Western powers. In view of the prospect that such an ultimatum would be rejected, the Soviets may move obliquely, endeavouring to make it increasingly impossible or unprofitable for the Western powers to remain on; for example, by interfering with the slender communication lines between Berlin and the Western zone, taking further action towards splitting up the city, bearing down on non-communist political parties in the Soviet sector, etc . . .

> Our Berlin position is delicate and difficult. Our withdrawal, either voluntary or involuntary, would have severe psychological repercussions which would, at this critical stage in the

European situation, extend far beyond the boundaries of Berlin and even Germany. The Soviets realize this full well.

Next day Murphy reported the beginning of the fulfilment of his own prophecy. The Russians wanted to assert a right, which they did not have, to enter Allied trains on the railway between Berlin and the West. They notified the Western Allies that their telephone engineers could no longer maintain repeater stations at Weimar and Magdeburg which were important for telephone traffic between Berlin and the West. On 2 April Murphy reported:

> While their [the Russians'] present actions are part of a larger and more ambitious programme, there is in our opinion nothing to be gained by hasty offers of concessions. Obviously our logistical situation in Berlin is unfavourable and the British and French supply situation is thin. However, there have been no interruptions thus far in commercial freight traffic to Berlin. Food for two million-odd Berlin residents, supplied by the United States, the United Kingdom and the French from the West, thus continues to be available.

That evening Clay telephoned to Washington and Washington telephoned to Secretary of State Marshall (who happened, by one of those accidents which bedevil the diaries of diplomats, to be in Bogota) to say, hopefully, that he thought the position could be held.

> Clay states [said Washington] that they can continue under present conditions indefinitely and he strongly recommends that this course be followed, even though it will require a substantial increase in air transport. We believe that any compromise proposal would play into Soviet hands and have a seriously adverse effect for the Western powers throughout Europe. He does not favour the evacuation of American dependants from Berlin.

On 13 April Murphy cabled Washington to say that he thought the Control Council was defunct but that the United States should take no steps to dissolve it because it was technically the 'badge of German unity'. He foresaw the continuation of Russian harassment of the Western garrisons in Berlin but was not sure whether this would lead to a denunciation of the agreement under which the Western powers were there. 'There is, of course,' he continued, 'the practical feature of food supply for the three Western sectors of Berlin with a population of about 2,300,000 who are now fed with food imported from the West. I am sure that the Soviet Union will avoid action to cut off this important item until the last moment.' Murphy also said he was afraid that in view of what he called 'the unfavourable logistics' the United States' determination to maintain its position might be vitiated.

At about this time (mid-April 1948), Winston Churchill – then Leader of the Opposition – intervened in the Western Allies' discussions with a much more bellicose proposal than any of them had considered. He thought that the time had come to tell the Soviet Union that if it did not withdraw its forces from Berlin and Eastern Germany to the Polish frontier, the Allies would 'raze their cities'. In support of this argument, Churchill said that in his view, when and if the Soviet Union developed the atomic bomb, war would become a certainty. The time to strike was when America had the bomb to herself. Churchill also suggested that the Western Allies should harass Soviet merchant shipping, meticulously examining their crews in all Western ports and annoying them if they sought to use the Suez and Panama canals.

The US Ambassador Lewis Douglas, who had heard all this in London, reported to the Under-Secretary of State, Robert Lovett, in Washington: 'You know better than I the practical infirmities in the suggestion. They cover quite a wide range, including the political.' He described Churchill's suggestion for harassing Soviet ships as 'the strand of straw disguised as a club'. Ernest Bevin was equally discouraging.

By the end of April the Western Allies' observations of the behaviour of the Soviet representatives in the Berlin Kommandatura which, unlike the Control Council, was still meeting, led them to believe that the Soviets were no longer interested in any serious attempt at four-power government of the city.

On 29 April there were difficulties over the Kommandatura interpreters. There was trouble about the agenda. The Soviet delegation stopped even trying to reply to points raised by the Western members. There were even some insults. Colonel A. I. Yelisarov, the Soviet Deputy Commandant, said that the nervous system of the American Deputy Commandant, Colonel William Babcock, was going to pieces. Mr Warren M. Chase, a member of Murphy's staff who was present, said that Colonel Babcock's nervous system seemed destined to outlast Colonel Yelisarov's. There was much laughter, but none of it Russian. There was no laughter at all at the 29 May meeting of the Kommandatura, which was even chillier.

On 2 June the Western Allies (after a brief hesitation by the French) agreed to set in motion the programme which would lead to the abolition of the Reichsmark and the launching of the Deutschemark in Western Germany. But before any of these measures could be put into effect, Colonel Yelisarov walked out of the Kommandatura in Berlin, never to return.

It seems to have been a petulant meeting and it lasted for about thirteen hours. At 10.45 p.m. on 16 June, after a fruitless discussion of a British proposal for a general wage increase, the American Commandant, Colonel Frank Howley, said he was going home and would hand over to his deputy. At this point, Colonel Yelisarov gathered up his papers, rose to his feet and led the Russian delegation out of the room. It was the end of the Allied four-power government of greater Berlin and the beginning of the end of the unity of the city itself.

A divided currency means a divided country, but by Friday, 18 June 1948, the creation of a second German currency was not so much the cause of German partition as the signal that partition was complete. On that Friday, after the banks had closed and at an immense press conference in Frankfurt, the British and the Americans launched the Deutschemark on a flood of confident oratory. The currency would be backed not by gold but by 'the German people's industry, their tradition of hard work, and the promise of Marshall Aid'. The new money would be available on Sunday, 20 June. Saturday would be a bank holiday. The Reichsmark would cease to be legal tender at midnight on Saturday. Old notes and coin denominations of one Reichsmark and below were to remain in circulation, but at a tenth of their face values. (This was in order to maintain the necessary volume of small change.) There was to be a moratorium for all debts until 26 June. An inventory of real property was to start immediately in order to try to minimize the advantages gained by hoarders of scarce goods and to prepare the ground for the introduction of some form of capital levy at a later date. The Western Allies said that they recognized that social and economic injustice was a problem which affected the whole structure of German society and that its solution must therefore be a German one.

This announcement resolved the uncertainties and anxieties which, in recent weeks, had transformed forty-five million thrifty West Germans into desperate spendthrifts. Saturday would be their last chance to convert their Reichsmarks into whatever goods were still available on a black market which was practically closing down. The British and the Americans took no special steps to prevent Reichsmarks being transferred into the Soviet zone.

The new currency was to be introduced in stages. As a start, every inhabitant of the Western zones was able to exchange sixty Reichsmarks for sixty Deutschemarks of which the first forty were paid out on Sunday at the local food offices and the remainder promised within two months. Every employer was to receive sixty new marks for each employee so that wages and salaries could be maintained at their existing level.

I reported that Friday from Frankfurt:

> It is clear that the complete division of Germany by what will amount to a customs and currency barrier along the western boundary of the Soviet zone will come as an unpleasant shock to many. Those Germans whose idea of currency reform was of a kind of painless financial panacea have already begun to realize how high that barrier will rise between them and their countrymen in the east . . .

That same day in Berlin General Robertson sent a letter to

Marshal Sokolovsky which said in part:

> I recognize the special circumstances of quadripartite govern-
> ment in Berlin and have no wish to disturb it unless this
> becomes unavoidable. As you know, we have striven for
> many months to reach a quadripartite agreement on a currency
> and financial reform which would apply to the whole of
> Germany. I am still firmly convinced that the only satis-
> factory course is to have financial reform on an all-German
> basis.
>
> Meanwhile, the economy of the British zone is suffering
> acutely from the evils of inflation and of economic stagnation,
> which our quadripartite proposals for financial reform were
> designed long ago to eradicate. I feel that I am not justified
> in waiting any longer before taking remedial measures. I have
> therefore decided to include the British zone in a scheme
> of currency reform to be introduced into the Western zones
> on Sunday, 20 June. Advance copies of the relevant laws will
> be sent to you.

The reaction was immediate. During the evening of Friday, 18
June, the Russians stopped all passenger traffic from West Germany to Berlin by both road and rail. The Russian regulations,
which were issued late on the Friday evening and came into force
at midnight, forbade pedestrians, motorists, and rail passengers
to cross the frontier of the Soviet zone from Western Germany.
At Helmstedt, on the Autobahn, between the British and Soviet
zones, the Russian sentries refused to allow cars to continue their
journeys eastwards, and turned back all save a single car containing
three Yugoslavs. Interzonal trains carrying German passengers
were halted at the Soviet frontier station at Marienborn and turned
back to the British zone. All the minor crossing places along the
frontier of the Soviet zone were closed simultaneously and greatly
increased forces of Soviet and German frontier guards patrolled
ceaselessly to prevent illegal crossings by Germans, who might be
currency smugglers or merely innocent citizens trying to find
their way home. Simultaneously there were electricity power cuts,
which the Russians attributed to a coal shortage. The suspension

Ferdinand Friedensburg

Part of the devastation that the Allies found in 1945: the Viktoria-Luise Platz neighbourhood

Ernst Reuter

of rail traffic was due, they said, to 'technical faults'.

Murphy kept cool. 'Certain of these measures', he told Marshall, 'are not unreasonable in view of the natural defensive action which might have to be taken to protect the Soviet zone from an influx of old currency.' However, he suspected that the West Germans, who had been obliged to change the old currency into the new Deutschemarks at the rate of ten RM for one DM, would be tempted to use their Reichsmarks in the Soviet zone where they were still legal tender. Murphy told Marshall:

> General Robertson telephoned General Clay this morning suggesting that a vigorous protest be made immediately regarding the new Soviet traffic regulations. Clay replied (it seems to me correctly) that it would be better to wait for two or three days because the regulations themselves are not immoderate, stating his opinion that were the situation reversed we on our side would have been required to take rather similar precautions.

Murphy's first reaction – that the Soviet measures were temporary and designed only to protect the East German currency – proved wrong. At 5 p.m. on 20 June the Russian guards at Marienborn stopped an American military freight train commanded by Major Lefevre of the US Army, and, to emphasize their point and their determination, removed a rail in front of it. To interfere with German interzonal movements was one thing. To interfere with Allied movements was more serious.

Meanwhile in Warsaw the Russians had been informing their East European allies of what they had already done and of their plans to do more. This, according to French sources, was the main purpose of a meeting of the Foreign Ministers of the Soviet Union, Albania, Bulgaria, Czechoslovakia, Yugoslavia, Poland, Romania and Hungary. (At this stage Yugoslavia and Albania still attended meetings of the Eastern bloc Foreign Ministers.)

Publicly the conference issued a communiqué condemning closer economic co-operation between the three Western zones. But if the French sources were right – and they probably were – the Warsaw conference was also the occasion on which the Soviet

Union secured the support of its East European satellite governments for its actions against Berlin. The conference, which lasted two days, ended on Thursday, 24 June.

But already, by cutting the electricity supplies and by stopping all rail traffic between Berlin and the West, the Soviet authorities had used their two most effective weapons. By 24 June the economic siege of the Western sectors of Berlin had begun in earnest.

PART II

PART II

4
The Tension and the Break

During the afternoon of 19 June 1948, Flying Officer A. G. Weller of 46 Squadron, RAF Transport Command, got his orders while he was minding his own business in Oakington, probably the most peaceful town in Cambridgeshire, which in itself is possibly the most peaceful county in England. 'We were told to position at Bückeburg to do a P.19 Shuttle whatever that was. The Air Force does not explain things to you.'

In fact Flying Officer Weller, Navigator II Rance, and Signaller Evans were on their way to try to save 2·1 million Berliners from starvation, to sustain them for a year, and to help to accomplish a feat of siege-breaking which no one except perhaps Truman and General Wedemeyer of the United States, and Clement Attlee, Ernest Bevin, and Air Chief Marshal Portal of Britain believed possible. Stalin, with seventeen divisions at his disposal on the ground, had isolated the biggest city in Germany from all its sources of supply. Weller, Rance and Evans were not alone as they walked out to their Dakota in Oakington. Transport fliers all over the Western world were to follow them. The Berliners did not know it at the time, but careful pilots from a hemisphere were coming to their aid.

Lieutenant Gail Halvorsen of the United States Air Force got his orders in a swimming pool at Brookley Air Force Base in Alabama. The Air Force intercepted Captain Jim Huston at Hamilton Field, California, as he was on his way to Japan. He was a four-engine pilot. So Berlin needed him. So he went.

The Berlin airlift got into its eventually mighty stride in three stages. In the beginning there was the P.19 Shuttle in which Flying Officer Weller and many other British and Commonwealth pilots did the best they could with the aeroplanes they had. Also in the beginning there was a similar effort by the United States Air

Force in Europe (USAFE). Stage two began with the arrival of more and bigger aeroplanes from American bases all over the world, most of them C.54 Skymasters which could lift ten tons compared with the three and a half which could be shifted by Flying Officer Weller's Dakota. Stage three began with the arrival in Germany of General William H. Tunner, USAF, who was then the world's most experienced and expert organizer of air transport. From the end of July, when Tunner arrived, the airlift – as the military saying goes – really began to sing.

In June 1948, though, the diplomats, naturally enough, were having their doubts. No one had mounted such an ambitious airlift before. Clay still hankered after an armoured breakthrough on the ground:

> I am still convinced that a determined movement of convoys with troop protection would reach Berlin and that this might well prevent, rather than build up, Soviet pressures which could lead to war. Nevertheless, I realize fully the inherent dangers in this proposal, since once committed we could not withdraw.

In the meantime, on 26 June, he and General Curtis LeMay, the Commander of the USAFE, had ordered an initial airlift of 225 tons of supplies a day to be carried by 70 aircraft. Murphy reported to Marshall that with 30 more aircraft the supply could be increased to 500 tons daily. Of this, the United States and British forces would consume 50 tons daily. 'The balance', said Murphy, 'would be devoted to the needs of the German population.' But he admitted that the actual requirement for food alone for the West Berliners would amount to about 2000 tons daily. From Berlin the prospect that an airlift could succeed seemed remote.

That evening Murphy, for the first time, grumbled aloud about the awkwardness of the situation with which he, Clay and Robertson were being asked to cope.

'My assumption', he told Marshall with a trace of bitterness, 'is that when the Western powers accepted the Berlin arrangement [at Yalta] they did so with knowledge of the possibility of Soviet pressure. The unfavourable logistical situation has been obvious from the start. It results from a defective agreement negotiated by Mr Winant [US Ambassador to the Court of St James from 1941 to 1946] and others in 1944 in an outburst of faith and goodwill designed to induce the Soviet Union to work in Germany with the United States and the United Kingdom in some form of organization however faulty.' Urging his government to arrange with the British and the French for a joint protest at the highest level, Murphy said that among other reasons for making this protest, it had now become important to sustain the morale of West Berliners and indeed of Western Europe as a whole. His reasons were:

> The protection of those Berlin elements who oppose, and indeed manifest courage in preventing, Soviet domination of the largest municipal area of Germany.
>
> The encouragement of German resistance to communist domination of the 18 millions residing in the Soviet zone outside Berlin.
>
> The fact that an allied retreat from Berlin would amount to an acknowledgment of lack of courage to resist Soviet pressure short of war and would amount to a public confession of weakness under pressure. It would be the Munich of 1948.

The next initiative was a British one and came from Bevin and Robertson. On 26 June Robertson delivered a letter to Sokolovsky which said, in part:

> The interruption of essential freight cannot be held to be a measure necessary to protect the currency position in the Soviet zone . . . I wish to make it clear that, if they [the rights of transit] are not restored and if undue and avoidable suffering is thereby inflicted upon the German population it will be because I have been deprived by you of the means to sustain them.

On the same day, 26 June, Bevin said what he intended to do about Berlin:

1. The circular movement of telegrams from the Americans in Berlin to Washington and back to London must be eliminated. Instead, both the Americans and the British would exchange information in three places – Washington, London and Berlin – so that decisions could be made more quickly.

2. The Combined Chiefs of Staff in Washington (an Anglo-American committee which had been set up during the war against Hitler) and the Chiefs of Staff in London must make a joint, agreed assessment of the military possibilities.

3. The Allied authorities in Berlin should jointly assess 'the logistic problem of feeding the civilian population of Berlin by air or otherwise . . . all possible air transport should be promptly mobilized for the purpose of transporting as promptly as possible (particularly for the women and children of the Western sectors) concentrated foodstuffs such as dried milk, dried eggs and dried vegetables, as substitutes for similar natural foods formerly supplied by the Soviet zone and now, according to reports, cut off.'

4. The Combined Chiefs of Staff should try to arrange to send a force of heavy US bombers to Europe. This, Bevin said, would be evidence that the Western Allies were in earnest.

5. The Western Allies must exchange views urgently about the usefulness, or otherwise, of sending a joint note of protest to Moscow.

The next day, 27 June, Marshall agreed warmly with Bevin's proposals. On 28 June, President Truman agreed as well. But, after consulting Defense Secretary Forrestal, he ordered Clay not to make statements referring to the possibility of war over Berlin. Truman said that if war were inevitable it should not be seen to have broken out simply over the question of two separate currencies in Germany. Washington agreed with Clay in his view that currency was not the basic Berlin problem. The basic problem was, as Clay had implied, quadripartite authority. After consulting the Defense Department, Marshall summarized a policy decision which was afterwards approved by the US Cabinet. The first three points, in Marshall's words, were:

1. We stay in Berlin.
2. We will utilize to the utmost the present propaganda advantage of our position.
3. We will supply the city by air as a beleaguered garrison.

On 1 July, President Truman backed Marshall in a statement to the Press. Bevin spoke in the same defiant terms in the House of Commons. For the first time publicly, Britain and the United States had committed themselves, their armed forces, and their money to sustaining the West Berliners by all possible means. At this stage, however, nobody could be quite certain what those means would be. Only Bevin had so far declared his faith that the airlift would succeed.

For the next few days the diplomats – British, American and French – brooded at length about the wording of a joint note of protest to be sent to Moscow. The soldiers, meanwhile, made a last attempt to persuade Sokolovsky. Generals Clay, Robertson and Noiret went to see him at 5.00 p.m. on 3 July to ask him about trains and roads. Sokolovsky's last explanation, given to Robertson, had been that there were technical difficulties on the roads and railways leading from West Berlin. Pressed for a statement, Sokolovsky said that when the current technical difficulties had been remedied he could not guarantee that others might not occur elsewhere. 'It is clear,' the Generals reported, 'that further action here by the three Western military governors would serve no useful purpose.'

To the Americans the outlook began to look bleak. In a telegram to London on 9 July, Marshall said that an airlift was 'obviously not a solution'. The next day Clay, while repeating his conviction that the Russians did not want war, suggested first that the Western Allies should offer to repair or remedy the 'technical difficulties' or, second, to send an armoured convoy up the Autobahn to Berlin. 'There is, of course,' he told Washington, 'an inherent risk in this course since once this convoy crosses the border it is committed to the movement to Berlin.'

By 14 July the Western Allies had sent their note of protest to the Soviet Union and the Soviet reply had arrived in the Western capitals. It was stern, accusatory and unyielding. It contained an offer by the Soviet government to 'secure by its own means adequate supplies for all greater Berlin', something which would have meant an effective Soviet take-over of West Berlin.

Bevin reacted like a lump of granite. He said that the Western Allies had no need to bestir themselves to draft a reply to a note like that. What the Western Allies must do now was to build up the airlift. He also wanted to know when the American bombers would be arriving in Europe.

Marshall agreed: 'We concur with Bevin that Press reports of the Soviets' intention to furnish food and possibly electricity, presumably on their terms, do not alter the basic issue of our position and rights in Berlin although they are undoubtedly intended to influence our airlift and may provide a pretext for insistence upon cutting down this method of supply.'

These were the tortured anxieties of joint diplomacy. Two days later, on 22 July, the military realities began to take shape. The National Security Council, meeting in Washington, decided to reinforce the airlift with seventy-five C.54 Skymasters and to authorize the construction of a third airport in Berlin, at Tegel in the French sector.

The Berlin airlift was the brainchild of two cunning old warriors – General Albert C. Wedemeyer of the United States Army, and Air Chief Marshal Sir Charles Portal of the Royal Air Force. They were old friends. They knew what they were talking about, Wedemeyer in particular because he had been the US Army's Theatre Commander in China during World War II and had been supplied by air – for there was no other way – across the Himalayas from India.

Portal had had no difficulty in persuading Attlee and Bevin that an airlift would work. Wedemeyer's task was harder. The alternative to an airlift was General Clay's plan to force a passage through to Berlin from the British zone, using tanks if necessary and confronting the Russians on the ground. What Wedemeyer knew and Clay did not was the strength of the Soviet Army in Eastern Germany and in Poland. 'Our forces', Wedemeyer wrote in a letter to the Commander of Langley Air Force Base, 'would have been annihilated.' And he foresaw the possibility that Western Allied citizens in Berlin would be 'marched off to the salt mines in Siberia'. Wedemeyer was in charge of plans and operations for the US Army. He read his Intelligence reports carefully. And he refused to accept a plan which he knew was bound to fail.

In practice there were five men who decided to mount an airlift. They were Attlee, Bevin, Truman, Wedemeyer and Portal. Of the five, Attlee and Truman were the decision-makers; they were also the two who were most alike. Neither could be bothered with detail. Both were men of precise and determined decision. Having decided on a course of action they expected that it would be carried out.

Wedemeyer and Portal were military men of great distinction. Portal had commanded the RAF for a long period. He knew his job. He was accustomed to being obeyed. And he knew what aeroplanes could do and what they could not do. Wedemeyer was a commander of vast experience – a tall, calm American soldier – who had lived through many tense times. The man they appointed to run the airlift – General Tunner – was their chosen technician – the Western world's supreme air transport specialist.

Wedemeyer addressed himself to the forbidding task of persuading his superiors that he was right and they were wrong. He went first to the Assistant Secretary of the Army, William Draper, who agreed with him. The two of them then went to the Secretary of the Army himself, Kenneth Royall. Royall was inclined to accept Clay's proposal. Wedemeyer flew to London in search of an ally and immediately found one. Portal had been contemplating an airlift already and had, indeed, organized Flying Officer Weller's P.19 Shuttle. But it was obvious to both Wedemeyer and Portal that the RAF could not support Berlin on its own.

Reinforced by Portal's decision and advice Wedemeyer returned to Washington to put his case to the Joint Chiefs of Staff and then to President Truman. He said it was ludicrous to think that the US Army could make a showing against the Soviet Union at that time. If Clay's plan were carried out the Russians could simply create more blockages on the Autobahn or the railways. They could carry on 'in this Fabian tactic for an indeterminate length of time'.

An airlift, on the other hand, would be feasible. Wedemeyer said he knew this because of his experience in China. And he knew that General William H. Tunner who had organized the airlift over the Himalayas would be the best man to organize an airlift to Berlin. The President agreed with him. The Chief of Staff of the US Air Force, General Vandenberg, was told to get on with the job.

At first Vandenberg was less than enthusiastic. The US Air Force (which had hived off from the US Army only one year previously) did not relish the prospect of denuding its Pacific Ocean bases of their transport aircraft. For a while there existed in Washington an extraordinary paradox. The Army was keener than the Air Force to mount an airlift. But Wedemeyer had persuaded the President and the President had spoken, and he was after all the Commander-in-Chief of all US forces.

Wedemeyer had not, however, persuaded Vandenberg of the need for General Tunner. Vandenberg said that anyone could run an airlift and that the prestigious General Curtis LeMay, the Commander-in-Chief of USAFE, would be competent to do it. Wedemeyer, who could not very well interfere in Air Force appointments, held his peace but watched with care the airlift's progress. After a fortnight both Wedemeyer and Vandenberg came independently to the same conclusion. The airlift was not shifting enough freight. The equipment was being under-utilized. With only the Harz mountains to hinder them between Frankfurt and Berlin, the pilots were delivering less than the pilots on the 'hump' had been able to deliver across the world's highest mountain range – the Himalayas. One night in the last week of July at Fort Myers, where the Generals lived, Vandenberg told Wedemeyer that he had sent for Tunner.

When the careful pilots arrived in Berlin they did not greatly like what they saw. This was the view from the cockpit of the approach to Tempelhof, the main base in the American sector, Lieutenant Halvorsen speaking:

> As we came in looking for this place all we could see were
> bombed-out buildings all around. Then we spied this grass

field – it seemed more like a pasture than an airfield – and came over the homing beacon and sure enough it was Tempelhof . . . We came right on over the top of an apartment building and over a little opening in the barbed wire fence and there we were. It kind of reminded me of the feeling that a crop duster would have in western America, landing on a highroad or in the pasture he's dusting.

The pilots' next problem was weight. All aircraft flying into Berlin carried enough fuel to enable them to return not just to Frankfurt or Celle but to a more distant alternate airfield in case the ones in West Germany were weatherbound. One American pilot, flying a C.54 Skymaster, flew from Frankfurt to Berlin, was unable to land because of weather, was again unable to land in Frankfurt, and eventually carried ten tons of coal to Marseilles in the south of France.

Because the aircraft had to carry enough fuel to do this if necessary, they were obliged to land in Berlin at weights which were abnormally heavy. 'If you pulled off your power like you're used to doing after an eight-hour overseas flight, then the old thing would sink like a rock,' as Halvorson put it.

Another disagreeable experience was accommodation. An Australian pilot, Jack Cornish (now an Air Vice Marshal), started flying Yorks into Berlin on the first day of the airlift, worked a twelve-hour shift beginning at either 4 a.m. or 4 p.m., and flew three round trips to Berlin in every shift. 'The ad hoc arrangements at Wunstorf meant sleeping in crowded dormitories. With people continually on the move and aircraft operating throughout the night there was little chance of getting rest.'

American pilots had the same experience. The occupying forces who had got to Germany first had acquired all the best billets, all the best barracks, and all the best beds. General Tunner raised hell about it whenever he had time. But the airlift pilots never did get the same standards of accommodation as the occupying forces.

5
Seeing in the Dark

When General Tunner arrived in Germany on 28 July he did not like what he saw any more than had the pilots at Tempelhof:

> My first overall impression was that the situation was just as I had anticipated – a real cowboy operation. Few people knew what they would be doing the next day. Neither flight crews nor ground crews knew how long they'd be there, or the schedules that they were working. Everything was temporary. I went out to the Wiesbaden Air Base, looked around, then hopped a plane to Berlin. Confusion everywhere.

General Tunner has since expressed his philosophy in his book *Over the Hump* in a memorable condemnation of the cowboy spirit:

> The actual operation of a successful airlift is about as glamorous as drops of water on stone. There's no frenzy, no flap, just the inexorable process of getting the job done. In a successful airlift you don't see planes parked all over the place; they're either in the air or on loading or unloading ramps. Flying crews are either flying or resting up so that they can fly again tomorrow . . . The real excitement from running a successful airlift comes from seeing a dozen lines climbing steadily on a dozen charts – tonnage delivered, utilization of aircraft – and the lines representing accidents and injuries going sharply down. That's where the glamour lies in air transport.

General Tunner was quick to realize that the airlift would have to work under a single command if it was to function efficiently. 'Far more successful than the Russians in hamstringing the Berlin airlift were the same old bugaboos I had experienced in India – divided command for one, and conflict between senior officers dedicated to the technical and strategic functions of the Air Force and those of us who had built up some experience in air transport.'

Tunner dealt with the first problem jointly with the RAF. The Combined Air-Lift Task Force – CALTF – was an Anglo-American organization led by Tunner and Air Commodore J. W. F. Merer, RAF, as his deputy. The planning officer for the airlift was Group Captain Noel C. Hyde of the RAF.

The first principle enjoined on pilots by CALTF was that they must fly at three-minute intervals at all times. Although to begin with there were not enough aircraft to maintain a string of cargoes three minutes apart for twenty-four hours a day, the three-minute interval was ordained to allow the airlift to expand when more aircraft became available. Tunner insisted on three minutes because this meant that at Tempelhof a plane would land or take off (because they had to come back again for another load) at intervals of ninety seconds which was the shortest interval which could be reasonably maintained with the control equipment then in use. The interval at Gatow, a clearer field, was two minutes.

The second principle, laid down later, was that if a pilot was unable to land in Berlin at his first attempt, he must fly straight back to the West. This rule arose out of a dangerous incident on Friday, 13 August 1948, when Tempelhof suddenly became enveloped in fog and heavy rain. One pilot overshot the runway. Another could not see the threshold, landed too far down the field, was obliged to use his brakes fiercely and burst his tyres. A third missed the runway altogether.

With the field obstructed, the ground controllers stacked the incoming planes which were arriving at three-minute intervals one above the other in the sky above Berlin. Quite soon the stack extended upwards from 3000 feet to 12,000 feet. A C.54 carrying General Tunner as a passenger was in the middle at 8000 feet. Tunner remembers saying, unoriginally, 'This is no way to run a railroad.' He then ordered the entire stack back to Western Germany. Tunner was not really a martinet in the stupid sense of the word. But he could act like one.

'I stated publicly that I would reduce to co-pilot status any pilot who failed to land with visibility greater than 400 feet and a

55

mile, and that I would court-martial any pilot who did land with visibility less than 400 feet and one mile. I never did court-martial any pilot or reduce anyone to co-pilot status on these counts. I never had any intention of doing so in the first place, but the message got across.'

The third CALTF principle was that all pilots had to fly by instrument rules – that is to say as if they were flying in fog and depending on their instruments – whatever the weather. This ensured that all pilots would be flying under the same set of rules and principles at all times.

Finally CALTF forbade pilots to leave their aircraft in Berlin so that they would lose no time in taking off once their loads had been discharged. Flight clearances and weather forecasts were brought to the aeroplanes. So was the food which was served at CALTF's special request by the most beautiful girls in Berlin.

The aircraft on the airlift ate up spare parts like hungry pigs. A stock of windscreen wipers which should have lasted six months was used up in a fortnight. Because pilots were making so many landings in relation to their flying time the landing gear had to be replaced much more frequently than anyone had foreseen. Tyres and brake-drums had to be purloined and brought to Germany from all over the world.

The official secret history of Tempelhof Air Force Base, written by Earle Overolzer Jr, a Captain in the United States Air Force and the base historical officer, has now been released for publication by the Defense Department in Washington. Captain Overolzer's narrative for June 1948 ends with these words: 'It can be noted and felt throughout Berlin that the Russian attempt to close Berlin to all ground traffic has been thrown back into their own faces because of the wonderful response the air force has given. The German people are grateful and appreciative of the entire operation. On the whole it has brought out a form of worship and admiration towards the Americans from the German people.'

One characteristic of a careful pilot is that he makes his job sound easy when it is not. Few Berliners can have realized the

Louise Schroeder

Trummerfrauen working in Hagelberger Strasse

Vassily Sokolovsky

William Tunner

skills that were being used on their behalf and the risks being run to keep them alive.

When the airlift began the Royal Air Force was better equipped and qualified to navigate in bad weather than the USAF. The RAF had developed radar landing and navigational aids which were much envied by the American pilots. All RAF and British civilian aircraft carried a navigator and most of them carried instruments based on high-frequency radar. Moreover the RAF navigators possessed the instruments and the training to be able to navigate without any electronic aids at all. If every electrical system in the aircraft went bad and if the sky was clear they could if necessary revert to the navigator's last resource, the sun and the stars. All sorts of things can go wrong with a radio compass, a radar set, or an automatic position finder. But nothing can go wrong with Arcturus. Even if the aircraft's power-supply fades into insignificance the stars will still be there.

The USAF was in a much less fortunate state. All that the American pilots had to help them find their way were a magnetic compass, a radio compass, and a somewhat undependable, fairly low-frequency radio link with the ground. A radio compass is not really a compass at all, in that it ignores the North Pole. It will, however, point towards a radio beacon provided it has been accurately tuned to the radio beacon's frequency; and provided that the beacon is within range. When the airlift began, the American pilots in the south corridor – one of the three agreed access-lanes to Berlin – which was more widely used by them than the northern one, had to cling to the voices of the radio beacons with a faith equivalent to that of the early Christians in salvation.

The voices of the beacons amounted to no more than their call-signs in Morse. No one who flew the airlift can forget them. For most of the American pilots the point of departure from West Germany to Berlin was the beacon at Fulda. Fulda is the site of one of the most celebrated Benedictine monasteries in Europe. In the tenth century it was famous for its missionary work in Germany. In the twentieth it regained fame because of its radio beacon. American pilots flying out of Rhein-Main and Wiesbaden knew where they were when they flew over Fulda, because, having homed in on it, the radio-compass indication would reverse itself by 180° when they were over the beacon itself. The arrow, having pointed straight ahead, would reverse itself and point to straight astern.

Fulda was a point of reassurance. After that, however, uncertainty could prevail. The distance from Fulda to Tempelhof is 211 miles. In order to stay in the air corridor it was necessary to fly this distance without major divergences from the true course. But as often as not during the early days of the airlift there could be periods of forty minutes during which neither Fulda nor Berlin were audible to the Americans. This meant that for two-thirds of one hour, while flying at 170 miles an hour, a pilot might have no navigational information from the ground. What made matters worse, and what has always made matters worse for the navigator, was the instability of the medium in which he was operating.

The essential problem of all navigation – by sea or by air – is to solve a vector triangle. One side of the triangle represents the vehicle's indicated course and speed. The next side represents the course and speed of the airstream in which an aeroplane is situated or the tidal stream or current in which a ship is operating. The third side of the triangle represents the true course and speed of the aeroplane or of the ship. The third side is the one that matters and is described by seamen as true course over the ground and by American airmen as the act of 'killing your drift'. In theory killing the drift is a simple operation. In practice it is much more complicated.

USAF pilots flying into Fulda from Frankfurt and Wiesbaden were accustomed to calculating the wind factor on their first leg and applying the same factor to the longer and uncertain journey from Fulda to Berlin. This was the best that they could do, because no one in the Soviet zone of Germany was going to tell them the wind direction and speed on their route from Fulda onwards. When it came to killing the drift, all that the American pilots had to go on – in the beginning – was the drift they had experienced at the start of their journey. Which was not by any means always the same as the drift they were going to encounter in the corridor, which was only thirty-two kilometres wide.

For American pilots flying the southern air corridor from Fulda to Berlin, the ultimate hazard was a break-down in communications with the ground along with a break-down in directional equipment. One particularly unfortunate crew lost first of all directional guidance on the compass and then suffered a malfunction of the radio to the ground. They were flying over an apparently limitless overcast, they could not accurately determine their headings, and their fuel was beginning to diminish. After a while however, they found a hole in the overcast and descended through it to find – to their relief – an airport. So they landed, and found themselves in Prague.

Having landed they were at once welcomed warmly by the Czechoslovakian Air Force, wined and dined and put up for the night. However it was not long before the United States Military Attaché in Prague told the crew that the sooner they got out of Czechoslovakia the better. At three in the morning, again, he repeated his advice, saying that the Russians were on their way to arrest the aircraft and its crew. This impelled the Americans into action. They took off in a hurry for Wiesbaden and arrived there, with their ten tons of coal, early in the morning. The Military Attaché reported later that none of the Czechoslovakian fliers who had entertained the Americans so amiably had been seen or heard of since.

This was, however, an isolated incident. For most of the time, which means 99% of it, American pilots did not have systems failures and were guided confidently into Tempelhof, Gatow or Tegel. Lieutenant Halvorsen was and is a faithful admirer of the radio compass. 'Tune the station and get a good signal, put it on automatic, and the needle will come round and point like a bird-dog – right at that station. And you home in on the station if you keep the needle pointed directly at it.'

But, many things could go wrong. Halvorsen remembers:

In the late summer of 1948, thunderstorms were still active and we were headed on a night flight into Berlin. We were just getting close enough to Berlin to start to pick up the radio signals, and because of the violent weather we'd been in we really weren't sure we were in the corridor. But we weren't worried too much about it. There were not going to be any Yaks [Soviet fighters] up there to get in our way because they were more a fair weather air force. So we were not worried about being intercepted, it being dark and really bad weather. But we were sincerely worried about where we were. As the signal on the radio compass got stronger we started to get an indication and then as it got clearer and clearer suddenly the radio compass deviated about 30°. We had been briefed that the Russians had a station on the same frequency, and that we had to be extremely careful. Well this went on and on and we couldn't get a fix. Old John Pickering who was my co-pilot – a Mobile Alabaman, we'd flown many thousands of miles together – was a kind of non-flappable kind of flier. I have seen him in situations before and he never got excited and this one didn't excite him either. We just couldn't find our position. Finally, working the radio compass, he reached for his head set, not in a fit of anger, just picked it up sort of in a manner of resignation and hung it up on a hook, looked at me and said, 'Those Russians shouldn't do that.' In fact, I think he said, 'Those damn Russians shouldn't do that.'

We flew on for five or ten minutes. I wasn't going to ask him to try it again, because he had done his best. And as we went on five or ten minutes he picked it up again and said, 'Well, maybe they're off the air.' Finally he was able to get a signal and then we double checked over the radio range and made a range let down and came in to land.

Halvorsen and Pickering were not the only crew to encounter and surmount problems like that. The installation of ground control approach radar in September 1948 made all the difference, as far as the Americans were concerned. With radar in Tempelhof the man on the ground could tell the pilot where he was, the direction in which he was heading, and – if necessary – what he ought to do. Lieutenant Halvorsen speaks appreciatively about radar-control:

> The radar brought us down between the buildings, right over that graveyard as we got lined up with the new runway. And the buildings, as we knew, were above us by the time we got into a landing position.
>
> With radar the fellow could pick you up about half-way to Berlin and say, 'I've got you on radar', and his voice is calm no matter what the weather. We had by then high-frequency communication and we didn't have to trouble with thunderstorms cutting out our coverage . . . And he'd call you in the middle of a thunderstorm and say, 'Well, Big Willy, you're right over the Elbe river, you're looking good, you're coming right along and things are looking good at this end.'

It was, says Halvorsen, just like someone patting you on the head.

The ultimate result of ground control by radar was the totally blind landing. GCA – Ground Control Approach – enabled the man at the airport to tell exactly where the plane was, its altitude, its speed, and its position. The man in the hut at the end of the runway now knew better than the pilot what the latter ought to do. This produced a new and psychologically revolutionary change in the relations between pilots and ground controllers. The man who was flying the plane, who had hitherto been the master and decider of what to do next, had to submit to the judgement of somebody on the ground who knew more than he did. To most pilots the surrender of the decision-making process did not come easily, but, fairly soon, most pilots accepted it.

With GCA it was possible to make landings in zero-zero visibility which, to pilots, means that you cannot see upwards or downwards or laterally either. Captain Huston describes how to carry out a landing in 'zero-zero' visibility:

> All you can do is follow the instructions of the ground control operator, be precise in your headings and your altitude, your rate of descent, and when he says you are over the end of the

runway, you've got to trust him. Cut your throttles, ease your airplane down like your tyres were eggs and just drop it on in and go back to your directional equipment and follow the directional heading of the runway all the way down until you can turn off.

Captain Huston and many others did this skilful thing time and again in order to keep the airlift rolling.

Navigation was not the only hazard. Flying Officer Weller encountered and overcame a problem which was peculiar to the airlift. The RAF rather than the USAF handled most of the west-bound traffic from Berlin to Western Germany. The loads carried varied from electric light bulbs – a Berlin export – to orphans. And the orphans brought with them difficulties of their own. The worst moment in Flying Officer Weller's long and distinguished flying career came in bad weather over the Soviet zone just before Christmas, 1948.

We had brought a load of children from Gatow to Lübeck. Normally there was a courier, an adult sent with the children, but my load for some reason was without this courier. It wasn't a very good day. It was instrument flying most of the way back, not rough, just murky. Everything went all right until we got into the blind approach pattern at Lübeck to make an instrument approach to the runway . . . We had just turned on to final approach when the aircraft started to go into a fairly violent nose-up attitude and I trimmed forward and pushed forward on the stick. I had to take a bit of power off as well. We were in cloud on instruments, not very high up, it would probably be only 1200 feet. I shouted to the wireless operator to see what was wrong. He opened the passenger door and found that nearly all the children were clustered at the rear end of the aircraft. He gesticulated and shouted for them to come forward and they got the message. I was able to retrim the aircraft and put some power on. I had missed the runway by this time and settled down into making another instrument approach pattern to pick up the runway again. What had happened was that, getting towards the end of the journey, one child had wanted to go to the toilet and the others had made a line. Which is always the way at children's parties. But I got them down all right.

The Hastings Mark I, which became one of the mainstays of the RAF contribution to the airlift, was regarded, like the C.46, as a 'tender' aircraft. RAF pilots who converted from Dakotas to Hastings tended to dislike what they had got. The Hastings was a splendid load-carrier but it gave its pilot very little help. It was difficult, according to Weller, to persuade a Hastings to calm down. All aircraft have two sets of controls – the main ones governed by the control column which the pilot holds and a subsidiary set of what are known as 'trim-tabs' which the pilot can set to counteract the effect of any factors like a maldistributed load which might make the aeroplane want to climb or to dive. The Hastings Mark I did not, on the whole, respond in a civilized way to trim. Worst of all, because of its reluctance to respond to trim and because it lacked a natural longitudinal, or fore-and-aft stability, a Hastings Mark I pilot was obliged to use both his hands on the control column when landing. This meant that he had no hand free to adjust the power. Which meant that he had to ask someone else to adjust the power for him. Which meant, finally, that there was room for misunderstanding or mishearing. In the worst case that Weller remembers his flight engineer reduced power to virtually zero during a final approach to the field at Schleswigland. They got away with it, but only just.

Another problem was the lack of repair facilities in Berlin. There was no room to service aircraft or for the maintenance engineers to live. Tunner decided that any USAF aircraft which lost an engine on the way into Berlin would have to be flown out empty and on three engines back to West Germany. This difficult task was entrusted to the Instructor Pilots of whom Captain Huston was one. A three-engine take-off for a four-engine aeroplane is an unpleasant undertaking in any case. Neither the RAF nor any respectable airline would sanction it for a moment.

What you have to do is lighten the aeroplane as much as possible, feather the propeller of the dead engine, test and run up the other three, and then reduce the power on the engine opposite to that which has died on you to a speed and power output which is virtually minimal. You can then commence a take-off using the other two engines which will balance each other until (in the case of the C.54) you have reached a speed of sixty knots by which time and speed the rudder will become effective. At this point you can bring in the third engine without which there will not be enough power for an actual take-off. Captain Huston, who did this difficult thing many times, says: 'About the time that your nose-wheel breaks ground you can bring the third engine into full power. The C.54 takes off very well empty on three engines. However if you lose another engine you have trouble.'

6

The Crowded Berlin Air

The construction of Tegel Airport was one of the triumphs of the blockade. (For the location of the three airports in West Berlin, see the map on pp. 132-3.) It was built in the French sector close to the French headquarters on a parade ground that had been attached to the former Hermann Goering barracks. There was a lot of sand and earth to shift. Four sandhills between ten and twelve metres high had to be removed. And there were only four bulldozers.

But there were also 19,000 Berliners who turned up to work night and day at Tegel. They started digging on 5 August 1948 and on 5 November the first American C.54 was able to land on the new runway. No airport had been built so quickly. Tegel now is one of the best equipped and largest aerodromes in Germany and carries virtually all the commercial traffic between Berlin and the West.

But it was clear from the beginning that the safety of aircraft using Tegel would be endangered by the transmitting towers of Berlin Radio, the East German radio station for Berlin and the surrounding country. The French Commandant, General Ganeval, who had served his time in Buchenwald concentration camp, warned the director of Radio Berlin three times that his masts would have to go. The director did nothing. Instead the Chief of Staff to the Soviet Commandant raised objections. In the end General Ganeval simply demolished the masts. The Soviet Commandant, General Kotikov, pleaded with him afterwards. 'How could you do such a thing, mon Général?' he said. 'With dynamite, mon Général,' said Ganeval; and that was the end of the affair.

Even with Tegel, the Berlin airlift was an air traffic controller's nightmare. Tegel meant that there were three airfields in Berlin and by airmen's standards they were much closer together than was comfortable. The flight paths had to conform to three narrow air corridors, two for inward-bound traffic and the third for west-bound traffic. The trick which had to be performed, and had to be performed every three minutes for thirteen months, was to have aeroplanes land at intervals of three minutes on the three airfields or two minutes at Gatow. The worst problem was in the north. For the controllers there were six sources of supply for the northern corridor: by the time the airlift was into its stride the British and American air forces and British civil freighters were using six separate airfields in the British zone – Schleswigland in Schleswig-Holstein, Lübeck, Fuhlsbüttel in Hamburg, Fassberg, Celle, and Wunstorf in lower Saxony. The United States Air Force flew out of Fassberg and Celle and, to complicate matters still further, Sunderland flying boats of the Royal Air Force flew into West Berlin from Hamburg. The controllers were obliged to co-ordinate the traffic from all these fields so that they entered the corridor at the right time, the right height and the right speed to ensure that all the aircraft would arrive in Berlin at precise intervals of three minutes, and without running into each other.

In theory, therefore, the controllers' task was to feed a string of aircraft, whose economic cruising speeds differed quite widely, into the western end of the northern corridor at three-minute intervals, and to accomplish this by ordering take-offs from six different airfields. The air traffic control problem for the southern inward-bound corridor was simpler. There were only two airfields, Wiesbaden and Rhein-Main, the airport of Frankfurt, and they were used solely by aircraft of one type – the robust and dependable C.54, then the DC 4 Skymaster of the US Air Force.

Practice was, of course, different from the theory. Pilots could not simply do what the controllers told them and expect to arrive over the Berlin beacons exactly on time on every occasion. Winds can change, take-offs can be delayed. Instruments in aircraft can go lazy. Every pilot was given a time at which he had to be over the Berlin beacon to which he was destined. In the event, most pilots most of the time had to adjust their speed along the corridor so as to satisfy the rigorous requirements of Berlin air traffic control.

There were also strict rules about height separation. These changed from time to time but were always mandatory, and without them the airlift would have been impossible. Speeds were mandatory too lest aircraft should begin to overtake each other or to collide longitudinally.

At one time, for example, the RAF Yorks from Wunstorf were bidden to fly to Gatow at 160 nautical miles per hour and at a height of 3500 feet. RAF Hastings had to fly from Schleswigland to Tegel at 1500 feet. The RAF's Lübeck Dakotas had to fly at 5500 feet and the American C.54s from Fassberg at 2500 feet. These heights had to be maintained whatever the weather and whether the pilot liked the altitude or not.

The air traffic controllers brought order into the airlift by despatching 'blocks' or 'waves' of aircraft from each of the Western airfields at co-ordinated intervals. The objective was to have in the air at any one time the maximum number of aircraft that could be controlled and handled at the Berlin airfields. The organization which achieved this aim continuously for more than a year stretched far back into Western Germany. The flight paths from the Western airfields to the western end of the northern corridor were elaborately planned to avoid any possibility of collision. As a crow would fly the distance from Wunstorf to Berlin is not much more than a hundred nautical miles. But in order to avoid flight paths from other stations, the distance actually flown by pilots from Wunstorf to Berlin was 175 nautical miles which took them over three radio beacons in Western Germany before they could head for the Frohnau beacon in Berlin. Twenty miles from that beacon all pilots had to report their destination (i.e. which airfield), their height, their load, their time of arrival at the beacon. The airfield would then tell the pilot which runway to use, the surface windspeed and direction, and give permission to descend to a designated height over the Berlin beacon. Once over the beacon the pilot would call the field again for permission to carry out his approach. It was a complicated ritual, but because the pilots had been rigorously trained and were accustomed to the disciplines of the air, the traffic flowed smoothly.

The orders for British pilots approaching the British airfield at

Gatow, as recalled by the Air History Branch of the British Ministry of Defence, read in principle as follows:

> On reaching Frohnau the aircraft would call Gatow and receive permission to carry out its approach . . . For a west landing the aircraft would then home to the Grunewald beacon and descend to 1500 feet but not below 2000 feet until south of Tegel airfield. At the Grunewald beacon it would make its final turn and change frequency to the final controller for the final approach and landing. As soon as visual contact was made the aircraft would change frequency again to the Gatow tower and complete its landing.
>
> For an east landing aircraft would home on the Huston beacon after leaving Frohnau maintaining a height of not less than 2000 feet. At Huston beacon the aircraft would turn and hold until six miles downwind of the runway, descending to 1500 feet. The aircraft would then make its final turn and change frequency to the final controller for its final approach and landing. Once visual contact was made the aircraft would change frequency to the Gatow tower and complete its landing.

To the pilots and navigators these and a host of other instructions equally detailed were the Ten Commandments. There was no room on the airlift for a Lawrence of Arabia. There was no room, even, for a General Custer. Everyone had to fly by the book and it had to be the same book. Otherwise you were lost and, worse, the flow of freight into Berlin would be interrupted.

The RAF used three main electronic systems for navigation. The first was Gee, a radio position-finding system which has now been refined to become the Decca navigator and the Loran Ocean navigation system. Gee depended on the measurement of very short intervals of time. If two transmitters on the ground send simultaneous signals and they both reach the aircraft at the same time, then the navigator knows that he is on a line which bisects the line joining the two stations. If one signal arrives before the other, the navigator knows that he is closer to the first station than he is to the second. If the two signals can be separately identified and if the time difference can be measured, the navigator has a position line. He knows, that is, that his aircraft is over a point somewhere on a line drawn on the map between the two transmitters. This line will be a curve or hyperbola. Two other transmitters or a third transmitter linked to one of the first two can generate another pair of signals offering the pilot another hyperbola. He can then be sure that his aircraft is on two position lines and that his precise position is where the two lines intersect.

Though RAF transport command aircraft were, generally speaking, equipped with Gee, its usefulness was limited east of the Iron Curtain, because of the distance from the ground transmitters.

The next electronic aid was called Eureka and was a radar direction and distance finder. The Eureka beacon at a pilot's destination transmitted a signal which, when displayed, told him whether his aircraft was on course and how far it was from the beacon. This instrument also depended on the measurement of very short intervals of time but was invaluable to navigators seeking to ensure a punctual arrival over the Berlin beacons. The trick was to calculate an estimated time of arrival as early as possible during the flight down the air corridor so that any changes of speed that might be necessary could be kept as small as possible.

The third electronic navigation aid carried by the RAF was a medium-frequency radio direction finder, a standard instrument in use since before World War II. But all three electronic aids could be jammed or otherwise interfered with by the Russians. Every navigator or pilot on the airlift had to be prepared to revert, if necessary, to the navigational basics — a map, a compass, a parallel ruler, a pencil, and a watch.

Seen in retrospect the statistics of the airlift represent a tremendous tribute to the pilots, to General Tunner and his Anglo-American staff, and to the fortitude of the people of West Berlin. But in achieving what they did, the British and the Americans surprised themselves. When the blockade began the problem was to feed 2,100,000 people, to keep them warm, and to sustain their morale by means of about 160 aeroplanes. All of them were small even by the standards of 1948. One hundred and sixty aeroplanes – about a hundred American and the rest British – seemed hopelessly inadequate.

General Clay summed up the problems:

When the order of the Soviet Military Administration to close all rail traffic from the Western zones went into effect at 6.00 a.m. on the morning of 24 June 1948, the three Western sectors of Berlin, with a civilian population of about 2,500,000 people [this estimate has since been reduced to 2,100,000] became dependent on reserve stocks and airlift replacements. It was one of the most ruthless efforts in modern times to use mass starvation for political coercion. Our food stocks on hand were sufficient to last for 36 days and our coal stocks for 45. These stocks had been built up with considerable difficulty as our transportation into Berlin was never adequate. We had foreseen the Soviet action for some months. We could sustain a minimum economy with an average daily airlift of 4000 tons for the German population and 500 tons for the allied occupation forces. This minimum would not maintain industrial output or provide for domestic heating and normal consumer requirements, and even if coal could be brought into Berlin in unlimited quantities, the electrical generating capacity in the Western sectors was limited because the Russians had removed the equipment of its most modern plant before we entered the city. Electricity from the Soviet zone was cut off when the blockade was imposed. The capacity which remained could provide electricity for essential purposes only a few hours each day, and even these hours of use had to be staggered for the various parts of Western Berlin. Despite these conditions we had confidence that its [Berlin's] people were prepared to face severe physical suffering rather than live again under totalitarian government, that they would endure much hardship to retain their freedom. The resources which we had within the theatre to defeat the blockade were limited. Our transport and troop-carrier planes, although more than 100 in number, were C.47s, twin-engined planes of about 2½ tons cargo capacity, and many of them had seen hard war service. The British resources were even more limited. There were no French transport planes available.

In practice five anxious months were to pass – July to November 1948 – before the airlift was bringing in the minimum of 4500 tons daily which the Western Allies considered to be necessary simply to feed the population of West Berlin, without providing for domestic heating, 'normal consumer requirements', and the raw materials needed by West Berlin factories if they were to maintain any sort of economic output.

7

The Mob Assaults Democracy

On 26 August 1948, after the airlift had been running for the best part of two months, but long before anyone knew if it would succeed, the East German communists and the Russians decided to divide Berlin politically and administratively, if not yet economically.

The Berlin City Council was still a single entity elected by all Berlin citizens. It met in the City Hall, the Neues Stadthaus, in the Parochialstrasse, a street in the Bezirk Mitte of the Soviet sector. The largest single party was the Social Democrats, or SPD. Along with the Free Democrats and the Liberals they outnumbered the Communists, or SED (which letters stand in German for Socialist Unity Party), by four votes to one. But the Soviet sector was policed and dominated by the so-called People's Police commanded by Paul Markgraf, the Nazi-turned-communist whose appointment as Police President for the whole of Berlin had been one of the Russians' first administrative acts when they captured Berlin in 1945.

The Russians and the East German communists were not prepared to allow this freely elected Council any longer to exercise authority in the Soviet sector. They decided to use straightforward coercion to prevent it from running the Soviet sector's services. They were prepared to hound it out of existence altogether or at least out of the Soviet sector. The instrument they chose was the Rentamob, an organized crowd of communist agitators who molested the Councillors on their way into the City Hall and who tried to prevent them taking their seats. Meanwhile the People's Police turned a blind eye.

This method was used experimentally and on a small scale on 23 June just after the airlift had begun. It was a small Rentamob and a half-hearted one and the Councillors were not greatly incommoded. All the same, the Speaker, Dr Otto Suhr, and the

Mayor, who was then Dr Ferdinand Friedensburg, took it seriously enough to propose a bye-law forbidding gatherings or demonstrations within a specified distance of the Neues Stadthaus. It was adopted on 29 June and was similar in form, content and purpose to the corresponding law which prevents unauthorized assemblies within a mile of Westminster.

But it was unenforceable. The first serious attempt to coerce Councillors or to prevent them from meeting took place on 26 August when a larger Rentamob molested Councillors in the Parochialstrasse while the People's Police stood idly by. An even larger mob tried again on 27 August but, again, was not up to the job. The third and final attempt took place on 6 September. This time the demonstrators actually broke into the building, occupied the Council Chamber, and took over the rostrum themselves. They were directly assisted, on this occasion, by the People's Police. Herr Markgraf was there in person and so (for the record) was Herr Wagner, the Chief of the Security Police in the Soviet sector, and Herr Eggebrecht, who was responsible for the maintenance of law and order in the Bezirk Mitte. These three men, backed up by a powerful contingent of People's Policemen, presided over an operation which was designed to ensure that the mob should get its way.

The Council was due to meet at twelve. The mob arrived at eleven in trucks, in small groups, and marching in columns. They began by breaking the glass in the entrance doors to the City Hall, overpowering the janitors, and occupying the entire Council Chamber, including the Councillors' seats and the public gallery. They laid violent hands on newspapermen. Dr Suhr, who was one of the few Councillors who actually managed to get into the building through the back door, reported afterwards that it was impossible to move in the corridors for the press of demonstrators. To his credit Dr Suhr waited half an hour to see if the crowd in the street would go away. 'Under these circumstances,' he afterwards told the City Council, 'no meeting was possible in the Neues Stadthaus. It would have been a mistake to try to sit there, quite apart from the likelihood that the majority of Councillors would not have been able to get in.' He formally adjourned the meeting and called another one for 7.45 that same evening at a Students' Hall of Residence in the British sector.

The demonstrators were not, however, content simply to crowd the Councillors out of their rightful place of assembly. The Leader of the Socialist Unity Party, the SED, Herr Karl Litke, was not, of course, molested. Instead he was allowed to have his say in the Council Chamber where he conducted a kind of mock Parliament in which he denounced from the rostrum the members of all the other parties. The Chamber, then being full of demonstrators, naturally applauded him. At about 2.30 in the afternoon they left, singing the Internationale. By then the People's Police had entered the Neues Stadthaus where they questioned many witnesses including pressmen, arresting some. There were fifty-nine arrests altogether. Forty-six of those arrested were policemen from the Western sectors who had been drafted in to try to protect the Councillors and who had a perfect right to do this. Some of them spent the night in the office of the American Liaison Officer with the City Council, where the French provided them with champagne and the British with Marie biscuits. At the adjourned meeting in the British sector Dr Suhr justified his decision to move the meeting westward, saying that, 'If we do not want to jeopardize democracy we cannot allow ourselves to be made fools of for ever.'

Only one Councillor objected. He was Dr Brandt (not to be confused with Willy) and he represented the East Berlin Christian Democrats, a party which had already been absorbed into the Soviet system as a sort of tame showpiece, an extra marionnette whose presence on the stage was supposed to show that democracy existed. Dr Brandt said that he, too, had observed the goings-on in the Neues Stadthaus and saw no reason why a meeting should not have been held. 'Any politician who has his point of view', Dr Brandt said, 'ought to be able to present it in situations which are not altogether pleasant.' Dr Brandt then challenged the legitimacy of the adjourned meeting and left the hall without waiting for an answer.

It came from the large, boisterous, and effective Councillor Franz Neumann of the Social Democrats. He said that Dr Brandt had been among the agitators at the City Hall that morning, that Dr Brandt and others had, that morning again, seen fit to use the political methods which had been made fashionable by the Nazis in Germany in the years 1928, 1929 and 1930.

To most Berliners the effect of the assault on the City Hall was shocking and immediate. The infant democracy which they had nurtured with pride since World War II had been set aside with the same brutal disregard for the democratic principle as Hitler and Goering had shown towards the Reichstag at the end of the Weimar Republic. Their ancient community which had existed as a unit since 1307 had been divided politically (though not yet economically) into two hostile factions. In East Berlin, where people had no option, the reaction was sullen resentment; in West Berlin it was indignation followed by an upsurge of democratic fervour. No one knew on 6 September 1948 whether the airlift would succeed or fail. No one knew whether those Berliners who stood up to be counted for democracy and freedom would be sent to Siberia or not.

Three days later on Thursday, 9 September three hundred thousand Berliners, which is to say one-seventh of the entire population of West Berlin, grandmothers and babies included, gathered in front of the Brandenburg Gate to protest against the siege of the City Hall. They were addressed by the leaders of all the West Berlin political parties. Although, because of the immensity of the crowd, not all of them could hear what was being said, their mood was unmistakable. They were there to bear witness to their brotherhood with the East Berliners, to their detestation of policemen or demonstrators who broke up elected assemblies, and their aching desire to preserve the freedoms they had been given only two years earlier. It was a town-meeting on an enormous scale, with people climbing the trees in the Tiergarten to get a better view of the steps of the ruined Reichstag where the speakers stood; and with those too far away from the public address system to make out what was being said clustering round cars equipped with radios. It was a meeting which brought out the orator in Willy Brandt and marked the beginning of his public service to West Berlin and Western Germany.

It was not, however, a rabble-rousing occasion. Its climax was a march from the Brandenburg Gate to the Allied Kommandatura building along a route parallel to the boundary between the British and Soviet sectors. Even so there were only two incidents. Some demonstrators went through the Gate into the Pariserplatz in the Soviet sector (where they still had a perfect right to be) and stoned a truckload of People's Police in the Dorotheenstrasse. The police replied with gunfire, wounding at least ten and, it is believed, killing two others. One demonstrator began to climb the columns of the Brandenburg Gate in an attempt to tear down the Red Flag which flew from the top. An intrepid Soviet army jeep tried to penetrate the crowd to bring a relief sentry for the Soviet War Memorial which lies just inside the British zone in front of the Reichstag. A first attempt to overturn the jeep was frustrated by the British Military Police who pointed out that Russian privates were not responsible for the deeds of Stalin. But when the Russians tried to return to their own sector the jeep was, in fact, overturned. Considering the size of the crowd and its emotions, however, the demonstration must be considered to have been orderly.

When the crowd, or a large part of it, reached the Allied Kommandatura building they were met by a duty watch of three American soldiers – a junior officer, a sergeant, and a private first-class. As the procession hove in sight with all West Berlin's leading politicians at its head, the officer asked his sergeant: 'Who are all these people and what do they want?' The sergeant said: 'It beats the hell out of me, Lieutenant.' I, who had preceded the march, more to be near a telephone than for any other reason, said that they were anxious for the Western Allies to guarantee their liberties. The lieutenant, with commendable dignity and presence of mind, accepted the petition on behalf of the Western Allies, the free world, General Clay, and President Truman.

This monster parade, for that is what it was, was the first concerted expression of the West Berliners' unspoken and unwritten alliance with the Western Allies and of their determination to stay free if they could.

***

76

In spite of the events of 6 September the Parliament of All Berlin was not altogether finished. The officers of the Council stayed where they were, led by a redoubtable retired Senator, Otto Theuner. At first there were no more Rentamobs. It seemed for a while as if the East German authorities were prepared to leave them alone as they were only the administrative officers. But this did not last for long. On 12 December Friedensburg was told to clear the Neues Stadthaus offices. Although the possibility of his arrest was as real as it always had been, Friedensburg went back to the Bezirk Mitte to help Theuner do the job.

Friedensburg, along with three other Councillors – Margarethe Ehlert, Valentin Kielinger and Friedrich Haas – had also been the last to leave the burning ship in the Parochialstrasse on 6 September. They had even insisted on being thrown out of the building, so as to leave no possible doubt about the communists' responsibility for dividing Berlin. The City Council stayed in being but was from then onwards representative of the three Western sectors only. But the Councillors refused to admit, even by implication, that the communists had a right to divide Berlin. They refused to set themselves up in a substitute City Hall in the West. Instead, they gathered in the Schoeneberg Town Hall. They still maintain that their rightful meeting-place is the Neues Stadthaus and they meet in Schoeneberg only as guests of that borough.

8

The Quality of Life Blockaded

During the blockade life in West Berlin was overshadowed by cold, hunger, darkness and noise. People could not keep warm because the power stations needed all the coal. The food rations were only just adequate. The power cuts, which resulted from the shortage of coal, were prolonged. The noise of the airlift never stopped, or if it did people became alarmed. At any one time for thirteen months there were at least three heavily-laden aircraft on their final approach to the three Berlin airfields. Tegel and Tempelhof, unlike Heathrow and John F. Kennedy, are located in the middle of the city. The noise in Berlin in 1948 and 1949 bore no comparison to the noise which now arouses so many protests in New York and west London.

The winter cold of 1948-9 was a severe experience. Berlin is a city of Central Europe. It lies in the plain of the Mark of Brandenburg. The only windbreak between Berlin and Siberia is the Ural mountains and the Polish frontier is only forty minutes' drive from Karlshorst in East Berlin. The nearest piece of sea, the Baltic, is not blessed by the Gulf Stream and much of it usually freezes over.

The cold of the winter was made worse than it would otherwise have been by the weakening of those buildings which had not actually been destroyed. It is difficult to heat a house if the windows have been cracked and there is no glass with which to mend them. To withstand the cold the West Berliners received a weekly ration of coal which they were able to take home in their shopping bags but a shopping bag half-full of coal does not suffice to keep a family warm for a week when it is snowing.

In practice, and because they are resourceful people, the Berliners went foraging. There was timber to be had on bomb sites. There was coal-dust to be salvaged on the airports where coal-sacks had spilled a little of their contents. In the last resort there were trees to be felled. The West Berliners shivered but not because they were dismayed.

In spite of all these problems and privations no one is known to have died of cold in West Berlin during the winter of 1948 to 1949. Nor is it known that anyone died of hunger. Rations were short but they were dependable. The main deprivation, compared to what had gone before, was that it became difficult if not impossible to obtain fresh vegetables from the Soviet zone. In a modest way the Mark of Brandenburg is a market-garden, brought to fruition by the Huguenots; it has always provided Berlin with fruit and vegetables, especially asparagus, and, above all, potatoes to which the Berliners are singularly addicted.

Before the blockade began the West Berliners were able to draw on this, their traditional market-garden, for supplements to their meagre rations. Between 1945 and 1948 the start of the asparagus season in the Soviet zone was greeted in West Berlin with the same sort of enthusiasm which, in France, celebrates the arrival of the first of the New Year's Beaujolais. The start of the strawberry season was a similar event. These happy anniversaries did not, however, survive during the blockade. West Berlin housewives, venturing into East Berlin to visit greengrocers (as they still then could), were harassed by the People's Police. The police would even confiscate potatoes.

Of all the West Berliners the housewives were called upon to make the greatest sacrifice. What has often been forgotten is that during the blockade the grass was greener on the Eastern side. There were more vegetables. There was more food. There was more electric current. In the autumn of 1948 the East Germans and the Russians offered all West Berliners the chance to share in these comparative delights. West Berliners had the chance to take up East Berlin ration cards which then were more generous than those which were valid in the Western sectors. Out of 2·1 million West Berlin residents only 20,000 accepted the offer and many of them later rejected it and returned to the West. But the West Berlin housewife's main problems were to feed her family, to keep them warm, and to keep their clothes clean. It is a problem too familiar to bear repetition but in a situation in which power cuts prevail over the periods in which electricity is on the problem becomes appalling. Candles became pearls beyond price. So did vacuum flasks. Without their help it was impossible to keep coffee hot during a power cut. Without heat, also, there could be no laundry. Berlin housewives used to get up in the middle of the night in order to wash and iron their husbands' shirts during the period when the power was on. It is difficult to do all these awkward things and remain cheerful. Yet the Berlin housewives succeeded.

There was also the question of illumination. A big, modern city does not realize how dependent it is on electric power until the lights go out. In West Berlin during the blockade the lights went out daily. The power cuts were drastic, but well-organized and not unfair. Kreuzberg was rarely worse off than Spandau. The Berliners reverted to candles; not that candles were plentiful. Nor did they give as much light as many of the interesting devices which the West Berliners constructed in order to be able to see their way around their own homes. There were hand generators for electricity. There were perilous gas-lamps. One way or another the Berliners contrived to produce for themselves enough light by which to read the newspapers, of which there were ten.

The Western Allies took pains to fly into Berlin – along with the coal, the flour, and the candles – enough newsprint to keep a free press going in West Berlin. To some Berliners this seemed to be an amazing objective, but there was unanimity between the British and American authorities that the West Berliners should have as many newspapers as they were prepared to support and buy. This was seen as an important democratic exercise. Diversity of news sources, cost what it might, was essential to a democratic experiment.

Although Britain and America – the two supplying powers – were determined to sustain West Berlin as a viable community they were also concerned to evacuate people who might suffer if they stayed there. There were two identifiable groups: orphans and young children, and sufferers from tuberculosis. During the blockade the Royal Air Force flew thousands of children to West

Germany where they could expect better living conditions. The United States Air Force flew about 1500 tuberculosis patients to West Germany. Faced with this requirement, airlift pilots unloaded coal and took on orphans.

The statistics say that 15,426 children were flown out of West Berlin to West German reception centres, either private or public. Most of them went to the British zone, most of the rest to the American zone, and 968 to the French zone. In all cases, however, they were cared for by the Berlin charity organizations and by the International Red Cross.

The blockade was punctuated by tragedies. Seventy-six people lost their lives on the airlift, most of them British and American fliers. The majority of these had been trying to reach Berlin in what airmen call 'marginal conditions'. Whenever an aeroplane crashed the West Berliners mourned. When two Dakotas crashed on the same day – 25 July 1948 – the mourning was general. The people of Friedenau turned out in their thousands to show their respect for the dead and their gratitude. West Berlin now has established a fund for the education and care of the dependents of those who died. The seventy-six casualties were sustained during one of the most intensive air operations that the world has known. By all the standards known to the civilian airlines the accident rate was minimal. But the Senate and people of West Berlin have resolved that no dependent of any of the seventy-six should go wanting.

The pilots delivered the goods. The city fathers and the Western Allies had to distribute them. The problem was immense. The authorities had to try to distribute fairly meagre rations of food and fuel to a besieged population of 2·1 millions. West Berlin, in those days, was about the same size as Saint Louis, Missouri; or Cleveland, Ohio; twice the size of Glasgow and half the size of Denmark. What made the task harder was that the population of Berlin contained many people with special needs and deserving special help. A large proportion of the West Berliners, probably as much as 56%, were women and many of these were war-widows or wives awaiting the return of their husbands from Soviet prisoner-of-war camps.

The main responsibility for this daunting exercise in fairness – for distributing to each Berliner according to his or her needs – rested on the small, strong shoulders of Frau Louise Schroeder, Berlin's first female governing mayor. The Berliners were lucky to have Frau Schroeder. She believed that a stitch in time saves nine, and that the time to prepare for the bad weather was while the weather was good. During her term of office she laid the foundations for a rationing system more equitable and more efficient than the Germans had known for a long time.

During the last months of the Third Reich the German rationing system had broken down to the extent that the ration cards were not always – at some periods rarely – honoured, so that people lost faith in rations altogether and headed, furtively or otherwise, towards the black market. Frau Schroeder and her successors did not succeed in abolishing the black market altogether. On the other hand they restored faith in rations. The rations would be small, even minute, but they would be there. This, alone, raised morale among the Berliners. The British, whose rations always turned up during the war, have no conception of the despair and insecurity engendered by a rationing system which does not work. In West Berlin, thanks to the municipal authorities and the Western Allies, it worked extremely well.

The West Berlin housewives had to come to terms from the beginning of the blockade with the unwelcome realities of dehydration. Real potatoes, for which the Berliners have an extraordinary appetite, weighed too much and were virtually banned from the airlift. Saccharin was lighter than sugar. All West Berlin's meat was boned before it left West Germany to save weight. Virtually every foodstuff from bread to coffee, to an unlovely substance called 'nourishing material', was on the ration. To supplement the rations West Berlin was bountifully supplied with Vitamin C which weighs hardly anything.

Even so there were extras. There were special rations for diabetics, blood-donors, nursing mothers, and the very old. Democracy was nourished too. When West Berlin went to the polls on 5 December 1948, to elect the new West Berlin Council, the presiding and returning officers were given special rations (including five grammes of precious coffee) to ensure that they would remain alert throughout the long day. By Christmas, when the Allies felt that they had a little room to spare on the airlift, there was chocolate, even, in a special Christmas ration. By Easter there was not only chocolate for the children (again as a special treat) but seventy-five grammes, no less, of coffee for the grown-ups. But the conspicuous merit of the Berlin rationing system was that hardly anyone in need was forgotten. Nor did any Berliner resent the special rations which were flown in for the animals in Berlin's prestigious zoo.

The real resentment arose over trees. Berlin is a city replete with woods. There is the Grunewald, the Forest of Spandau, the Jungfernheide, and there are many avenues and back gardens with trees in them.

On 7 October 1948 the Allied authorities – who had been monitoring the daily tonnages of coal carried by the airlift as carefully as a nurse takes a patient's pulse – told the governing Mayor (by then Ernst Reuter) that a lot of Berlin's trees would have to come down. The Western Allied Commandants, like Louise Schroeder before them, were taking thought for the morrow. At this time the daily deliveries by the airlift amounted to about 4000 tons, sufficient for the time of year, but only just. Berlin has a meteorological history of bad weather in November which could be expected to interfere with the airlift. Moreover the coldest part of the winter would come after Christmas. So the Commandants asked for 350,000 cubic metres of wood to keep the West Berliners warm in January, February and March.

There was an outcry. The City Council proposed to cut 120,000 cubic metres. In the end there was a polite compromise. The Commandants said that 120,000 cubic metres would be enough for the time being; but if the weather got worse the Berliners would have to consider felling and cutting out another 150,000 cubic metres. In the event the weather spared many trees. West Berlin got by on 120,000 cubic metres of firewood and most of the trees were saved.

The transport of coal was one of the most crucial and difficult problems to confront the airmen. Coal-dust is bad for the insides of aeroplanes, so the coal had to be damped before it could be loaded, which made it heavier than it would otherwise have been. In the airlift's first full month, July 1948, coal imports by air amounted to only 43,000 tons compared to the normal July consumption of 325,000 tons. It was certainly not clear then, and did not become clear until a good deal later, whether West Berlin could survive the winter without freezing to death. In the beginning the coal was shipped in sailors' duffel bags of which the US Navy had a plentiful supply. Later it was shipped in paper sacks. Either way the transport of coal by air was a painful business but one which, after an initial attack of amazement at the thought of carrying coal at all, the pilots accepted as normal.

The Allied Commandants and the West Berlin City Council appreciated the pilots' point. Not an ounce of coal was wasted in West Berlin in the winter of 1948–9. On 19 July 1948, as a first draconian measure, the authorities confiscated from virtually all West Berlin coal consumers, every scrap of coal they had in their cellars in excess of their expected needs for the next ten days. This applied to schools, factories and even hospitals, but not to the public services like gas, water, and the power stations. The unanimous decision of the Western Commandants and the West Berlin City Council was that the power stations, the pumping stations of the Berlin waterworks, and – taking third place – the gas works must be looked after first. The worst contingency that they could imagine in the energy sector was a total and long-lasting failure of electric power. Eleven thousand tons of precious coal were transferred from Berlin's gas works to the power stations. There were five of these in West Berlin at Moabit, Spandau, Schoeneberg, Steglitz, and Wilmersdorf. Even then none of them could be regarded as particularly efficient – thermally speaking. They had been designed, years before, to consume coal from Silesia which was in Poland, whence no more coal was coming. Instead, during the blockade, they consumed West German coal and consumed it hungrily. Even so the power cuts were cruel. For long periods Berliners could only hear the radio news by going out into the streets to listen to the loudspeaker vans sent round by RIAS, the main Berlin transmitter in the Western sectors, whose name derives from its original title Radio in the American Sector. And most evenings the West Berliners had to read by candlelight.

There was a real possibility that thousands of Berliners, particularly older Berliners, could have died of cold. West Berlin's only defences against this catastrophe were the airlift of coal and the wood from the trees. Nor was the wood much use until it had been dried. Ferdinand Friedensburg, Louise Schroeder's immediate successor as governing mayor and a man of great courage and resource, conceived a third alternative. He was a mining engineer from Silesia. He knew, and he was right, that there ought to be deposits of lignite underneath Spandau. In fact there were deposits underneath Reinickendorf and Marienfelde as well. None of them had ever been judged commercial. Friedensburg simply said that these were not commercially-normal times and that it would do the West Berliners good to learn to be coalminers. Fifteen bore-holes were sunk in the hope that Berlin's inner-suburban lignite mines would be able to produce 500 tons a day thereby eliminating the need for fifty flights by American C.54s.

Friedensburg was right, to the extent that the lignite was there, but there was hardly any of it. Even in West Berlin's strained circumstances it would have been uneconomical to mine it. Friedensburg was subjected to a certain amount of mockery. From the West Berliners' point of view this was, perhaps, justified. It was as if the Mayor of New York had started digging for coal in Central Park, the Chairman of the Greater London Council had sunk a shaft in Parliament Hill Fields. Friedensburg was undaunted. He said that it was a pity that West Berlin did not, after all, possess reserves of lignite, but it would have been ridiculous not to look for them. A lot of careworn, coal-flying pilots agreed with him. So did the vast majority of West Berliners. No one now believes that Friedensburg made a fool of himself.

***

As the blockaded Berliners ate their dried potatoes an inspired and unlikely combination of American soldiers and German broadcasters reached the sound conclusion that the next best thing to food was accurate news and jokes. The result was the flowering of RIAS which was – and is – the best all-round radio station in Central Europe. RIAS is a many-sided thing (broadcasting some of the best criticism of Shakespeare that can be heard in Europe), but its first major task and triumph was to tell the truth clearly during the blockade and to make people laugh. On Christmas Day, 1948, when the outlook for West Berlin was about as black as it could be, RIAS launched a new programme which was to become a by-word not just in Berlin but throughout the Soviet zone. Eight inspired entertainers, led by Günter Neumann, gave the first of 148 episodes of *Die Insulaner* ('The Islanders'). Their main theme, which they maintained until the end, was that for some reason they could not fully understand, Berlin was surrounded by water. Neumann's gifted collaborators – Tatjana Sais, Edith Schollwer, Bruno Fritz, Ilse Trautschold, Jo Furtner, Agnes Windeck, and Ewald Wenck – were all Berliners or had become Berliners. Their humour was devastating. Their victims were everywhere. They persuaded cold and hungry Berliners to stop thinking for a while about the next meal or kilogramme of coal. And they made the Berliners laugh at everybody. They took the liberty (as it then was) of laughing at the occupying powers, Western as well as Russian. They laughed at the East German authorities and, above all, they made the Berliners laugh at themselves. Not many Germans have this gift – or not many had it in those days – but Günter Neumann did, so did *Die Insulaner*, and so – as matters turned out – did the Berliners themselves. *Die Insulaner* were a smash-hit throughout the blockade and for a long time afterwards.

But RIAS was and is much more than a joke-programme. There was the news, which went to the Soviet sector and zone as well as to West Berlin. There was also the task of reintroducing to Berliners the world they had not been allowed to inhabit since Hitler came to power in the 1930s. 'The war has left us defeated, and in a spiritual fog, but hungry for good and nourishing thoughts and full of curiosity about the world outside.' So said Friedrich Luft, RIAS's distinguished drama critic in one of RIAS's first transmissions in February 1946. For the Berliners, RIAS opened these doors and has held them open ever since. Outside Berlin, in the Soviet zone and in Czechoslovakia, RIAS listeners have had access for more than thirty years to some of the best cultural broadcasting in Europe. But RIAS has always been, first of all, a community service for the West Berliners. During the blockade, when the power cuts made it impossible for most people to listen to the radio all the time, RIAS would retransmit its programmes and the news from loudspeaker trucks around the city. They even built seats in the Schöneberg Municipal Park for listeners to sit on.

In its early days RIAS used to run a service called 'Where are You?' designed to help refugees from the East find their relatives. Seven thousand two hundred and sixty-eight did. When on 12 May 1949, RIAS joyously announced that the blockade was going to end, 400,000 people – nearly one-quarter of the population – answered RIAS's invitation to gather on the Rudolph-Wilde-Platz to listen to the liberty bell and rejoice.

Günter Neumann was a genius who died young but who was there when Berlin needed him. He had the opportunity to bring a freshness into people's lives which they had missed during the Nazi period. His genius – which was also Shakespeare's and is exemplified in such characters as Bardolph – was to make his audience identify the characters and to identify with them. After a while, when he tried to introduce new characters into *Die Insulaner* scripts, the listeners protested. They came to adore the familiar – the awful, pompous, stupid, hectoring East Berlin civil servant, the fiercely incomprehensible Russian professor who interrupted him, the two old ladies from the Kurfuerstendamm, poor Otto Normalverbraucher (which means Mr Average Consumer, who had a dreadful time).

All these people were brought alive and became part of Berlin's life and also of the life of the people in the Soviet zone. And never did the pace flag or the jokes go stale. In 148 performances *Die Insulaner* kept Berlin supplied with the one vital ingredient of life which Hitler, the war, and the Russians had kept from them – permission to laugh at anything, and particularly at authority. One of Neumann's best works was called 'I was Hitler's Moustache' – a title which happily and healthily anticipated the Hitler-biography industry of the 1970s.

When Günter Neumann died in 1972 at the age of fifty-nine the Berliners built a memorial to him on one of those artificial mountains made of rubble which they had been forced to build simply because there was nowhere else to put the debris of the war into which Hitler had led them. The mountain is in Kreuzberg, which is in many ways the jolliest part of Berlin though not the most beautiful. Anyway Kreuzberg, for a number of complicated and typically Berlin-like reasons, now has a mountain called *Die Insulaner* with a Neumann memorial on top. If the Berliners were pompous enough (which they are not) to put together a Roll of Honour of those who helped them most to survive the blockade the name of Günter Neumann would be on it, along with Lucius Clay, Louise Schroeder, Ferdinand Friedensburg, Ernst Reuter, Willy Brandt, General Tunner, and the airlift pilots. Neumann once wrote that the Berliners were rude to each other (as they occasionally are) only to conceal their sentimentality. This was kindly meant. And it probably comes closest to describing the Berliners' common fundamental characteristic. But what Neumann and *Die Insulaner* did was to make them laugh at themselves as well.

Above all, and brilliantly, RIAS has always told the news as it is and told it fast. There have been many crises in Berlin since 1945 – the blockade, which was a long one; the uprising of 17 June 1953, not just in the Soviet sector but also in the Soviet zone; the building of the wall in 1962. Finally, and not far away from Berlin, there was the Czechoslovakian uprising of 1968 and its suppression. RIAS rose to all these occasions. It was the RIAS man who had his cable cut during the assault on the City Hall in September 1948. RIAS men were the first to get arrested in the Alexanderplatz during the events of 17 June. RIAS was on the air before dawn on the Sunday that they built the wall. RIAS also monitored and retransmitted the radio messages that the Czechoslovakian railwaymen were sending to each other in an attempt to thwart the Russian invasion in 1968.

The man who began all this was an American colonel called Westerfield in November 1945. What has flowered and flourished ever since has been the expression of the spirit of Berlin on 303 metres. Half Europe can hear it and a lot of Europe does.

9
The Tons per Day

For West Berlin the vital indicator was the average number of tons flown into the city. Although the RAF never was, and never could be, as big a contributor to the airlift as the United States Air Force, it was nevertheless able to mobilize its resources more quickly. This was partly because Britain was closer to Berlin than were America's far-flung outposts – the Philippines are a long way from Europe – but partly also because Ernest Bevin insisted that the RAF should lose no time in putting forward its maximum effort. By July 1948 the RAF contribution to the airlift had already reached 90% of its maximum. But the figures for July, the airlift's first full month, caused the Western Allies much anxiety. The RAF flew in 937 tons and the United States Air Force 1289 making a total of 2226, a long way short of the required 4500 needed simply to feed the West Berliners.

August was a great deal better with the RAF flying in 1340 tons, the US Air Force 2376 and British civil aircraft 123 tons, making a combined total of 3839 tons. September was rather worse, with a total of 3654 tons; October, however, saw a substantial increase in the American contribution due to the arrival of more C.54s. The October figures were 1026 for the now combined RAF and British civilian aircraft and 3734 for the USAF, making an encouraging total of 4760. Between September and October, therefore, the USAF had managed to increase its contribution from 2395 tons to 3734 tons. But for the weather the airlift would have been even more effective.

Fog, snow and ice – but mainly fog – combined to make flying difficult in November and to reduce drastically the tonnages moved in that month. The British contribution dropped to 854 tons per day, the American to 2932. At 3786 the daily total of tons transported was lower than it had been in August when there were fewer planes. December was nearly as bad with an average daily airlift of 4563 tons (a total of 141,468·1 tons for the month).

For the Western Allies, and particularly for the Western sector Commandants, November and December were the anxious months. They were worried not so much about food as about fuel. The power cuts were frequent and maddening, but the Western Commandants' main worry still was the problem of keeping the Berliners warm. In October they had serious doubts as to whether the airlift could bring in enough coal to prevent the West Berliners – the elderly ones at any rate – from freezing to death. The Allies asked, or almost ordered, the West Berliners to cut down their trees.

From December onwards the daily tonnage lifted was always in excess of the 4500 tons which the Allied Commandants considered to be the minimum required to support life. Partly because of the climate, partly because the West Berlin power stations were antiquated and by modern standards inefficient, West Berlin turned out to need about three times as much coal – 1,586,529 tons – as food. The total for food was 538,016 tons. The other main import was diesel oil and petrol of which the British civilian airlines imported 92,282 tons, most of it during the winter. The main export was people. In the course of the airlift, 174,020 people were flown out of Berlin, most of them by the RAF. As Berlin grew accustomed to the blockade, industry revived and learnt many new ways of dividing its products into packages small enough to be flown out to the West. The RAF alone flew nearly 12,000 tons of freight from Berlin to the customers who were waiting for it in Western Germany.

By the spring of 1949 the airlift was running like a railroad. Daily tonnages frequently equalled 7000 tons. General Tunner decided that the time had come for a day of demonstration, for the big parade. He wanted to transport to Berlin in one day not merely a worthy 7000 tons, but much more.

His main reason for wanting to put on what he admits to having been a 'show' was that he assumed that the Russians were about to admit defeat and to abandon the blockade; and he could help to persuade them to do this more quickly by flying into Berlin in one day more than twice the daily tonnage required, so that they (the Russians) would realize that the blockade was not working any more.

Tunner had abiding faith in the ingenuity of all those under his command. He believed that if you involved 4000 people instead of 2000 in the business of getting as much coal as possible to Berlin you were likely to get many more new ideas because 4000 heads are better than 2000. So Tunner involved his entire command. Cooks were made to load coal. Generals were made to fly as co-pilots. Idleness was out of the question. Competition between squadrons became the order of the day.

Experience had taught him – on the airlift from India to China – that a very large, record-breaking total achieved on one day would always inspire the pilots, the loaders, the co-pilots, and the maintenance men to do better than they had been able to do before. Tunner, wise in years and experience, knew from the statistics from the airlift over the Himalayas that, however well you had been doing in advance of a record-breaking special day, you would do better after the day was over.

All of Tunner's expectations were realized. He had chosen the period for the all-out effort to coincide with Easter, as an Easter present to the Berliners. Between noon on Easter Saturday, 1949, and noon on Easter Sunday, CALTF pilots and crews, and loading and unloading crews, shifted 12,941 tons of freight into Berlin in 1398 flights. This was more than enough to supply West Berlin for three days. Moreover there had been no flying accidents, nor any hitch in the air traffic control. There had been no problem which CALTF had been unable to handle. Tunner, who had spent the final twenty-four hours commuting from one base to another, was at Wiesbaden when the last flight was about to leave. He remembers seeing an enthusiast running out to the last plane which would be able to reach Berlin before the noon deadline with a paint brush and a pot of red paint. He painted on the side of the waiting C.54 the vital statistics about fuel and flights. 'And then he ducked against the blast of wind as the pilot, with just a few seconds to get into the air, gunned his engines and headed for the runway.'

Tunner's decision to stage his 'Easter Parade' was clearly right.

Hindsight shows that the Russians were taken aback by the evidence that the airlift was capable of supplying within twenty-four hours three times as much in terms of tonnage and supplies as West Berlin needed. 'Whatever the cost, the airlift had done its job, and West Berlin was free. We had shown the world what free nations could do,' said General Tunner.

It is to Tunner's eternal credit that he promoted what he afterwards called the Easter Parade in the face of a good deal of opposition. The Commanding Officer of the United States Air Force in Europe, by now General Joe Cannon, had stood aside from the airlift operation which was, after all, the major operation conducted by the United States Air Force in Europe at that time. When Tunner decided to mount the Easter Parade, General Cannon was on leave in the United States. Tunner kept his plans to himself:

> I got the staff together and we began making definite plans. First, we decided on absolute secrecy. If we set a quota of, say, 10,000 tons – 50% higher than we'd ever done before – and then failed to bring it off the communists would crow over it.
>
> In spite of our secrecy, word of the intending event spread to USAFE and to Cannon's deputy, Major General Robert Douglas. Douglas called me immediately. 'I don't want to discourage you,' he said, 'but even if you have a lot of tonnage and then drop way off the next day, Joe's going to raise hell.'
>
> 'We are not going to drop off the next day,' I told him. I was sure of that. We had learned on the Hump that after a big all-out push the tonnage would of course decrease the following day when we returned to normal but it would decrease to a higher plateau than had formerly obtained.

The Easter Parade was a resounding success; it influenced the Russians and encouraged the Berliners and the British and American governments. And General Douglas's prediction that the airlift would 'fall flat on its back' on the day after the special effort turned out to be incorrect. The combined airlift task force succeeded where the politicians thought that it would fail. The

Easter Parade turned out not to be a flash in the pan. It was, instead, the prelude to yet higher daily tonnages of supplies shifted into West Berlin.

General Tunner was also right when he predicted that the airlift's obvious and shining success would discourage the Russians and induce them to end the blockade. Within days of the Easter Parade the Soviet Ambassador to the United Nations, Jakob Malik, approached the American Ambassador, Dr Jessup, in the corridors of the UN building in New York. The meeting was decisive but discreet. The Russians were offering to lift the blockade and to restore surface communications between West Berlin and Western Germany in return for the resumption of trade between West Germany and East Germany.

When the blockade began, the Western Allies had, as a natural measure of retaliation, imposed a trade embargo between their zones and the Russian. This impeded East Germany's economic development to an extent which was plainly serious. But though this had obviously affected Russian thinking, the Easter Parade was probably the decisive factor. The pilots had made the Russians look silly in the eyes of the world and – as the Russians seemed to fear most – in the eyes of their East European satellites. Every East German who listened to RIAS knew that the blockade was no longer working. Every East European who listened to the BBC or to the Voice of America received the same message.

The Malik-Jessup meeting was discreet to the point of absurdity. With the tactlessness with which diplomats often treat soldiers the State Department failed to tell Tunner or Clay. Clay, who first read about it in the newspapers, was understandably cross. Tunner was more tolerant. However it became known, the news was good. By 4 May 1949, eighteen days after the Easter Parade, the Russians, Americans, British, and French were ready to announce that the blockade would end on 12 May and that interzonal trade would be resumed.

It seems certain now with hindsight that the East Germans badly needed this trade. The East German steelworks were short of coking coal from the Ruhr. Silesian coal did not suffice. The

East German economy was stagnating, partly for lack of supplies from the West, while the West German economy, reinvigorated by the introduction of the Deutschemark, was expanding. The difference between living standards and the value of money in the Western and Eastern parts of Berlin was becoming obvious to all. Even under siege, West Berlin was a more prosperous place than East Berlin.

The political motives for lifting the blockade were at least as strong as the economic ones. The whole world could see that the Russians, with seventeen divisions on the ground, had suffered a moral defeat and, in particular, that the West Berliners were rejecting all the offers and temptations that the Russians had been able to lay before them.

In West Berlin 12 and 13 May were days of great rejoicing. Many East Berliners joined in too when it was safe for them to do so. The crowd which gathered at the Berlin end of the Helmstedt Autobahn was immense and joyful. Truck drivers were welcomed as though they were the soldiers who had raised the siege of Gloucester. People hung garlands on the unlovely steam locomotives which brought the first tidings from the West into West Berlin. Eleven months of hardship were forgotten in an afternoon.

Clay and Robertson, who had rejoiced as much as anybody, nevertheless insisted that the airlift must go on. Their first purpose was to build up reserve stocks in West Berlin in case the blockade was reimposed; their second to demonstrate to the Russians that the Western Allies were still suspicious. The continuation of the airlift was meant to be a sign that the Allies did not yet trust Marshal Sokolovsky. So the skies above Berlin did not fall silent on 13 May. The airlift continued until September, by which time it was actually hauling more coal into West Berlin than was coming in by rail or in barges.

One shrewd observer whose joy was muted was Robert Murphy. He pointed out that the Western Allies had received nothing much of diplomatic importance. The airlift had been a tremendous triumph, but it had proved only that a large city could be supplied by air, expensively, but indefinitely. But by building a bridge in the sky the Western Allies had, by implication, failed to insist on their rights of access by road and rail. The agreement which ended the blockade had left Berlin in the same position as it had been in before. Murphy was a true prophet. The airlift had certainly demonstrated that General Wedemeyer and Air Chief Marshal Sir Charles Portal had been right in saying that given enough aeroplanes and the men to fly them you could do anything – even if it meant feeding two million people and keeping them moderately warm through a nasty winter. But West Berlin's problem remained the same as it had been before. It was still an island. Communications between Berlin and the West were resumed over land and by water. But the Berliners' right to use them had not been clearly re-affirmed.

This meant that, although this blockade had been defeated, the Russians and the East German government could still find excuses to harass communications in many small and tiresome ways. They continued to do this over the years and although the results were annoying rather than fateful, the feeling induced in West Berliners was one of continuing insecurity. In other ways, too, the ending of the blockade turned out to be a less joyous event than it seemed. When the blockade ended West Berlin had been continuously in the news for over a year. Prime Ministers, Ministers, Congressmen, Members of Parliament, and even Bob Hope had arrived with the coal to cheer the Berliners on. Once conditions reverted to what passed for normal the world became bored. Berlin in trouble was front-page news; Berlin isolated but getting on with its business – which still was mainly reconstruction – was routine to the point of obscurity. The fact that Berlin was still surrounded by covetous enemies, still a long way from the Western zones of Germany, and still rent as a city by a relentless quarrel between dictatorship and freedom, passed unnoticed into history.

10
Pilots for Liberty

Captain Huston says that when he rode the radio beam into
Tempelhof for the first time, he reflected that on his last visit to
Berlin his instructions had been to bomb Tempelhof out of
existence, and that this was paradoxical. A man less careful in the
use of English might have called it amazing. For six years up to
1945 the British and the Germans had been trying hard to kill
each other. For a shorter period the Germans and the Americans
had been doing the same. And here was Captain Huston flying
an awkward route in the dark to save the people he had bombed.
Many other pilots, British as well as American, must have been
struck by the same reflection. Huston had exchanged a deadly
B.17 for a benevolent C.54. RAF pilots had exchanged Lancasters
for Yorks and Hastings. This time it was coal and flour instead of
phosphorus and high explosive.

The Berlin airlift did not, however, mean that the Western
Allies had changed sides. What they were doing – as Truman,
Attlee, Wedemeyer, and Portal saw the matter – was to defend the
cause for which Britain and America had already shed so much
blood. The Berlin airlift was mainly about liberty, about the West
Berliners' right to freedom and to choose the way of life they
wanted.

Because of this the West Germans' adherence to and enlistment
in the Western Alliance of free peoples became a possibility. The
airlift transformed the Western Allies, the pilots in particular, and
the West Berliners from ex-enemies into comrades in adversity.
The links and bonds which now bind West Germany into the
NATO alliance were forged in West Berlin, and in the skies above
it in 1948.

Apart from its miseries, indeed largely perhaps because of them,
the blockade was a unifying experience. No one who lived through
it can ever contemplate eating dried potatoes again. The British,

G   97 the Americans, and the Frenchmen who were in West Berlin that year will not easily forget the West Berliners just as the West Berliners will not easily forget their former enemies. The blockade transformed an occupied city into a fraternity. Out of that fraternity grew the conviction that Britain, the United States, and West Germany could join together in NATO, which stands above all for freedom. In this sense the blockade of Berlin may have been one of the biggest mistakes that Stalin ever made.

Adversity is a uniting force, as the British discovered during the war. Every housewife, British, American, French or German, who lived through the blockade knows a great deal about how to make the rations go further. Every journalist who was there is an expert at getting candlegrease out of typewriters.

There were also exhilarating visitations. Clement Attlee arrived modestly on a load of coal. Ernest Bevin, who hated flying, arrived as well. And an inspired director of the Berlin Office of the British Council called Guy Wint, a distinguished student of the Far East and a *Guardian* leader-writer, imported the Marlowe Society from Cambridge in two Dakotas on the grounds that if the West Berliners could not actually understand *The White Devil* they might at least appreciate the gesture. At first Wint was severely criticized and even mocked. He had, after all, deprived West Berlin of six tons of boneless meat. But Wint was right. The Marlowe Society played to packed, if uncomprehending, houses. 'There's nothing sooner dry than women's tears' translates easily enough; but 'I am in the way to study a long silence' is more awkward. In the event the West Berlin theatre-going public applauded Wint and the Marlowe Society because they appreciated what they rightly regarded as a hilarious British initiative. With friends as mad and carefree as the British Council how could Berlin lose?

But, Wint and Webster notwithstanding, the people who forged the strongest links were the pilots. All of them, probably, came to care for the West Berliners, but the man who usually speaks for them is Lieutenant Halvorsen, a deeply modest member of the Church of Latter Day Saints from Provo, Utah, who had fame thrust upon him when he became the first pilot to drop sweets to the West Berlin children. (You do this by making a handkerchief into a parachute, attaching the sweets to the parachute, and dropping the resulting package out of the flare chute of a C.54.) Halvorsen became known as the 'Sweets-bomber' and when he returns to Berlin on Air Force Day about 550,000 people turn up at Tempelhof in an attempt to shake him by the hand. He is only the symbol – as he would be the first to say – of all the other pilots who began to love the people they were feeding. But annually, even now, rather more than one-quarter of the population of West Berlin – men, women, children, and old-age pensioners – turn up to give thanks for the airlift. Halvorsen says this about the people he fed:

I try and think where I got my first impressions. I guess that happened on the very first flight into the city. We landed with the 138 sacks of flour and queued up behind one or two other C.54s to get on the apron where we were unloading in front of that huge hangar that Hitler had designed in 1933–4 and built in 1936, like an eagle in flight. We stopped and no sooner had the propellers stopped turning than our engineer opened the door and there were three or four Berliners standing right in that door. The truck was ready to back up by the time we stopped and was already backing by the time our props stopped turning. They looked at those sacks of flour and you could tell what they meant to them. I think that this was their ticket to freedom, that if enough of those sacks came through they'd be able to stay in Berlin, they'd be able to stay free, and they looked at us Americans as we came down between the sacks with respect and a smile on their faces, put their hands out, and gave us a slap on the back; and yet *they* were the heroes.

They were the ones who went home at night to bombed out places, as many Britons had done, and went home without enough to eat, took what meal they had for their families, and yet they were the ones that were cheering us on and here we had been enemies a short time before. It was a feeling that I've never quite had since, to see another human being that looked at you and you doing your job and nothing more.

I'd never quite had that feeling before that we were pulling together for something important. And as I met more of these people, and they would come with that truck every time we'd stop the airplane, that feeling was reinforced of working to a common worthwhile goal, to give food for kids, to provide medicine for the sick and the minimum kind of things that one needed just to live, to survive, not to be rich, just striving to be alive. Oft times there'd be some German children there with older people supervising them and bringing us flowers. I'd never had that happening before. Of course, in America we don't use flowers like they do in Europe, certainly not like the Berliners. But they'd bring flowers out. One day a father and his son brought me out a little coach – a handmade coach with horses, doors that opened – and he told me how long they'd worked on it, they wanted me to have that. A little girl brought out her very favourite teddy bear, her Berlin bear, and insisted that I take it and it was worn on the elbows and I put it on a string and flew it with me in the cockpit.

I love optimistic people. I like people that think it can be done, that it's worthwhile, there's something good in there somewhere, and they are that kind of people. They're brave, they live in the jaws of the tiger all the time. I think that I've never met such a group as the Berliners who were there at the end of the war, who toughed it out, who said, 'Look, we'll give everything we've got, we don't care if we haven't got anything but the clothes on our backs' – and that was literally true. They didn't reserve anything unto themselves. They said, 'You stick with us and we'll just give you anything we've got – and if that isn't enough we'll stay here with you or whatever else.' When you've got people with dedication like that you can't help but love them.

That spirit of freedom that the Berliners inherently had, I think, was strengthened. As the blockade hit they saw their chance to lose it and that's what was behind the expression of those volunteers that stood outside that airfield saying, 'If you need any more help, we're here.' And as they came in there to unload that flour and to unload that coal, the looks and the feelings that were exchanged, expressed more than any words or any picture or any sermon you could preach. I have a special feeling for them, I think they were the real heroes of that episode, their determination and their spirit sparked a return spirit in the Allies.

Gail Halvorsen is the last pilot in America who would claim notoriety or fame. Citizens of Salt Lake City and Provo are curious to know why the outside world is interested in Bishop Halvorsen of Provo. Puzzled enquirers in Universal City, Texas, want to know why strangers from London should be looking for Colonel Jim Huston. Huston now is a city father of Universal City. Halvorsen, of Norwegian descent, is a Bishop in the Mormon Church (which does not mean anything as prestigious as an Anglican Bishopric) but both are persons in whom compassion shines.

There are many other pilots, both British and American – probably at least 2000 – whose affection for the people they saved is equally intense. In the compass of this book I have been obliged to allow four pilots to speak for thousands. I would be surprised, however, if any pilot – RAF or Commonwealth or British civilian, or from the USAF, or from the US Navy – would violently disagree. The Berlin airlift was a mission of compassion. The people who flew it were skilful enough to make it succeed against all the odds but were also sensitive and intelligent enough to know that their purpose was to sustain the liberty of 2·1 million people who wanted to stay free.

The Diplomats Ruminate

Once General Tunner had taken charge of the airlift towards the end of July 1948, very few pilots had the time or the opportunity to explore the city they were sustaining or to meet the people whose liberty they were trying to preserve. General Tunner had decreed that pilots must either be flying or resting up to fly again. The people who had time to reflect upon and analyse the conflict that was developing between Britain and America on the one hand and the Soviet Union on the other were the British and American diplomats in Berlin, London, Washington, and Moscow. Their correspondence, most of which has now been published, shows that they were bothered by two problems. The first, a minor one, was the rickety state of France. America and Britain, Britain in particular, were anxious to ensure a united front between the three major Western powers in the face of the most serious Soviet threat that had developed since the end of World War II. The French were contributing nothing to the airlift, partly because of their preoccupation in Indo-China but partly also because of what seemed like irresolution.

At the end of July the US Ambassador in London, Lewis Douglas, explained Bevin's apprehensions to Washington: 'Bevin fears that he is doing his utmost to carry what he calls a fearful and a bankrupt France and that the pressure on him in the effort to maintain a united front among the Western European powers is a very great burden which he is trying desperately to carry.'

As winter approached the state of France grew worse. The government fell on 4 September and it was six days before another one could be formed under the premiership of M. Henri Queuille. During the interregnum Douglas wrote despairingly to Washington:

There is no government in France or at least there was none

this morning. My information indicates that Schuman [the retiring Prime Minister and leader of the popular Republicans who became Foreign Minister in the Queuille government] after experiencing difficulties forming a cabinet has told President Auriol that he either is unable to form a government or wishes to be relieved of the responsibility for forming one. When a government may be formed in France is hard to tell. After it has been formed, when it will be able to make a decision on this [the Berlin] question is still another matter.

The other problem – that of relations with the Soviet Union – worried the diplomats even more. The advice they were getting from the military was contradictory and, taken as a whole, unhelpful. General Clay did not think that the airlift could be sustained and said so. On the other hand the alternative which Clay favoured – an armoured thrust from the Western zones through to Berlin – was firmly rejected on 28 July by the United States Defense Secretary, Forrestal. He told the diplomats bleakly that the Joint Chiefs of Staff in Washington did not recommend the sending of an armoured convoy along the Autobahn to Berlin, 'In view of the risk of war involved and the inadequacy of United States preparations for global conflict'. Forrestal went on to say that 'contingency planning for an armoured convoy would go ahead in case every other solution were to fail or to have been discarded, and in case a new evaluation showed that the armoured convoy was likely to get through, and in case the United States decided that the risk of war for the Berlin cause was acceptable'.

For the policy-makers in London and Washington these were two pieces of depressing advice. Following quickly, a third and equally depressing telegram arrived from the US Ambassador in Moscow, Mr Walter Bedell Smith. He was convinced that even if the airlift did work it would not save Berlin:

Though the Western airlift, contrary to original Soviet expectations, probably means that real hunger can be staved off indefinitely, time is still working entirely in favour of the Soviets if they desire to make the position of the Western powers untenable. For besides the war of nerves against non-communist German elements, the economic life of the Western sectors cannot be supported by food alone. By now, it is apparent that the airlift cannot supply sufficient coal, other raw materials and consumption goods, or solve the problem of outward shipment . . . the Soviets must be convinced that they need only sit tight with the present blockade in order eventually to force the Western powers out.

To their considerable credit the policy-makers were undismayed by all this gloomy advice. Bevin, Attlee, and Truman were unmoved. Bevin, for one, was confident throughout. He told Ambassador Douglas that 'time is running in our favour', that the airlift augmented by the additional C.54s had in the past, and would in the future, continue to surprise and wear down the Soviets. Douglas reported to Washington that there could be no question whatsoever about Bevin's purposes and determination. He quoted Bevin as having said that 'the abandonment of Berlin would mean the loss of Western Europe'. But Bevin and Truman were not prepared simply to let matters take their course without raising as much diplomatic hell as they could under the circumstances.

On 3 August, all three Western Ambassadors in Moscow were received at the same time and at their governments' request by Stalin. It was a long and fruitless meeting, lasting two hours. Stalin said that the restrictions on travel had been caused by technical defects, but that there were additional reasons for them. Large quantities of equipment were being moved out of Berlin and into the Western zones, the Eastern zone was now vulnerable to the new West German currency, and the Western Allied decision had meant the division of Germany into two states. Because there were two states there were also two capitals – Berlin and Frankfurt. Since there were two states and two capitals, Stalin argued, Berlin could no longer be regarded as the capital of the whole of Germany, but as the capital of Eastern Germany. This being so, it was intolerable that a separate West German

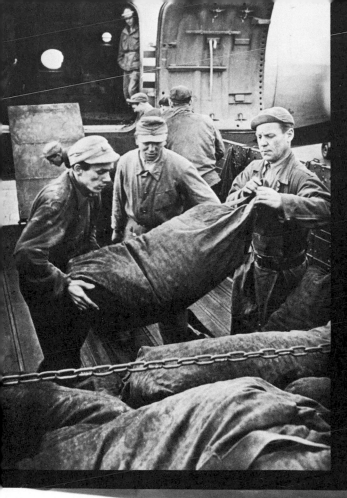

Unloading coal at
Tempelhof

Left to right: Lucius
Clay, Ernest Bevin,
Brian Robertson

Waving goodbye to a C47

The first rentamob demonstration against the City Hall, 1948

currency should be introduced in West Berlin.

Bedell Smith came away with the impression that Stalin and the Foreign Secretary, Molotov, who was also at the meeting, were ready for a settlement. Bevin did not share this view. Nevertheless, the three Ambassadors in Moscow kept on trying to sound out Soviet intentions. Smith of the United States, Frank Roberts of Britain and Yves Chataigneau of France had to endure the frustrating experience of being strung along by Molotov and one of his deputies, Andrei Smirnov, until virtually the end of August. At the end of the day the Soviet government offered, in effect, to lift the travel restrictions in return for economic control of the whole of Berlin. The Eastern currency would be the only valid tender. Regulation and 'emission' would be controlled by 'the German Bank of Emission of the Soviet Zone'.

Clay was the first to turn this down, Marshall and Bevin next. The Ambassadors soldiered on. Perhaps because of their efforts, perhaps because the Russians thought it expedient anyway, Marshal Sokolovsky accepted an invitation from General Robertson to a meeting of the four Allied Commanders in Berlin on 31 August, which by general consent was not regarded as a meeting of the Control Council as such, by then defunct.

They held a series of meetings, the first since the spring, but they could not reach agreement. The problems were currency, the travel restrictions and the unity of Berlin. The Western Allies suspected that Sokolovsky was going back on the limited agreements that the Ambassadors had reached in Moscow. Sokolovsky, like Molotov before him in Moscow, celebrated the start of every new meeting with a new objection. The three Western Commanders, showing commendable stoicism, kept the conversation going with the Russians well into the winter. Finally the Policy Planning Staff of the US State Department decided to dismiss from its mind the arid complications of the Bank of Emission and to review the situation properly. The result was a top secret paper called PPS 42 which said in part:

The Berlin situation poses for this government a genuine dilemma. The outlines of this dilemma are simple. On the one hand, every consideration of national interest, aside from the Berlin situation, indicates that we should not become involved in a war at this time. In the development of the European situation in general at this juncture a continuing deterioration in the communist political position in Europe will eventually make war unnecessary. Our own military position, furthermore, is less favourable today in relation to the Soviet Union than it can be expected to be in a year or two hence. Finally, both the military strength and the self-confidence of our Western European friends can presumably be considerably enhanced by a further period of progress towards a North Atlantic defense arrangement.

Thus, if we can avoid war at this time, there seems to be a good prospect: (a) that we may possibly be able to avoid it altogether (this is perhaps the vital difference between this situation and that of the French and British at the time of Munich), and, (b) in any case we may be sure that if it [war] has to come we will be in a better position to fight it a year or two hence than we would be today.

On the other hand, we must recognize that in the confidence and enthusiasm which our position has inspired in the population of Berlin and in the symbolic meaning which this situation has acquired as a test of strength and determination between East and West, we have factors of enormous importance. These factors militate against any unilateral Western withdrawal from that city which would involve surrendering the population of the Western sectors to communist oppression and revenge.

The paper went on to say that the West had so far been able to prevent the extension of the communist police system over any European peoples 'beyond the high water mark of the Soviet military advance during the war. To permit such extension now,' the paper continues, 'by the abandonment of our position in Berlin, even though the persons whom we would be sacrificing are Germans for whose fate we would have been very little concerned three years ago, would inevitably undermine confidence in us elsewhere in Europe and above all in such delicate and exposed spots as Vienna and Trieste . . .

'We have here one of the great recurrent imponderables of foreign policy, an emotional factor which may bear little logical relation to the practical considerations involved but which is of major unanswerable importance . . .'

PPS 42 also said:

> We must recognize that Berlin cannot be left indefinitely dependent on the airlift for its source of supply. It is not sufficient to judge the airlift from its technical aspects alone in estimating the length of time in which we can hope to supply Berlin by this means. We must also take into account psychological and political considerations. We must recognize that the population of a great city, particularly one which is in dire need of reconstruction on a grand scale, cannot get along indefinitely with just the absolute minimum of food and fuel. Sooner or later the sacrifices involved and above all the uncertainty itself, must breed discouragement and unrest and resentment even against ourselves.

PPS 42 seems to have been the main policy document which guided Anglo-American policy until the blockade was lifted on 12 May 1949. It was, in many ways, a prophetic document. It assessed the airlift as a gamble but as a gamble on which the British and the Americans were morally obliged to embark. It also foresaw accurately the nature of the tension which would inevitably persist after the blockade had been lifted. The tension between the Russians who had suffered a moral defeat and the Western Allies who had won a moral victory was sufficiently strong and enduring to make the unification of Germany impossible. It had probably been impossible from the beginning – that is to say from the time in 1944 when Roosevelt, Churchill, and Stalin had signed the Yalta Agreement – but the Russian blockade of Berlin in 1948 and 1949 rendered the division of Germany no longer even negotiable.

PART III

12

The Two Germanies Drift Apart

For the next four years from 1949 to 1953 West Germany and West Berlin, sustained by Marshall Aid, got their breath back – economically speaking – with extraordinary speed. When the Western Allied economists introduced the Deutschemark in Frankfurt in 1948 by saying that the new currency would be backed by the industry of the German people, they spoke prophetically. Though West Berlin, still isolated, did not recover as quickly as West Germany, it was able to benefit from the West Germans' rapidly growing prosperity. West Germany helped West Berlin much more generously and effectively than East Germany or the Soviet Union assisted East Berlin. The city became divided into an eastern part where austerity governed everything and a western part which became richer, busier, and happier year after year. The years between 1949 and 1953 were a period during which the contrast between West Berlin's prosperity and East Berlin's continuing poverty became more obvious month by month. In the East, the state department stores – or *Handelsorganisationen* (known as 'HOs') – had little to offer. In West Berlin the department stores gradually became filled with goods as varied, expensive, and exotic as anything that could be bought in the Rue de Rivoli, Fifth Avenue or Bond Street.

There was also a growing contrast between take-home-pay in West Berlin and in the East. Take-home-pay is the vital economic statistic which affects people in the most important ways. Bricklayers in West Berlin were earning more in real terms than bricklayers in East Berlin. Statistics, only some of which were dubious, showed that an East German worker would have to put in three times as many hours at work to buy a pair of shoes as his counterpart in West Berlin. The Deutschemark was worth four times as much as the East German Reichsmark. The contrasts were considerable and growing all the time.

What was worse, from the East German government's point of view, was that the contrasts could not be concealed. The East German authorities simply could not censor the news from the West – if only because RIAS and the other West German radio stations were audible everywhere and were broadcasting in a language common to both parts of Germany. A Romanian shoemaker could not necessarily discover whether he was better or worse off than his counterpart in Austria. But the East German workers knew very well how much their counterparts were earning in West Berlin, and it was a lot more than they were earning themselves.

In spite of remarkable achievements by the East Germans (it is arguable that they are the only people who have made collective farming work properly) the disparity between West Germany and West Berlin on the one hand and East Berlin and East Germany on the other continued to grow. Correspondingly, discontent continued to grow among the East German workers. Some of them moved to the West in search of better pay and better conditions. Others moved west because they wanted to live in freedom. Those who stayed behind became increasingly discontented. Inflation continued in East Germany. Take-home-pay became more and more inadequate to maintain standards of living. And when the East German government intervened to try to cure or retard inflation it did so with the minimum of tact. The dam of discontent finally broke in 1953.

The workers' revolt which broke out in East Berlin on 17 June 1953, was in favour of freedom and against a workers' state and a statutory incomes policy. On the wages front the workers won, against all the might of a police state and ten divisions of the Red Army. But on the freedom front they lost, and at the cost of many lives.

It all began on the Stalinallee, which is the Berlin end of the highway to Frankfurt-an-der-Oder, Warsaw, and eventually Moscow. Badly damaged by bombs during World War II, the Stalinallee was being reconstructed to house the East Berliners in flats worthy of the sons and daughters of a people's democracy. It was an immense project, conceived in the then fashionable architectural spirit of socialist realism. Thousands were working on it. The spectacle of industry was impressive even if the architecture was not. But it was this enormous construction site which was the scene of the beginning of an originally industrial protest in which the bricklayers of East Berlin gave the East German government the fright of its life.

Their immediate complaint was a government decision to raise the work norms by 10%; that is to say the bricklayers would have to lay 10% more bricks for the same money. Not unnaturally they regarded this as a 10% cut in wages – which it was, or would have been had they not challenged the government, the armed police, and the Soviet army successfully.

As so often happens the demonstration was sparked off by weakness and hesitation. The decision to raise the norm in the first place had been one muddled mistake. The decision to rescind the first order was another – and for the government it was nearly fatal.

There had been minor demonstrations on 15 June, a Monday, which had seemed to result – so far as the workers on the Stalinallee building sites were concerned – in a concession. There had been strong rumours as early as the previous Friday that the decision to raise the norms would be withdrawn. But the workers wanted confirmation and they wanted it early on the morning of Tuesday, 16 June.

At 9 o'clock an unfortunate, and perhaps uninstructed party functionary called Gutzlaff told the eighty workers who were building Block 40 on the Stalinallee that the norm would be raised after all. Gutzlaff's brief message broke the dam. Block 40 downed tools and took to the streets. Within the hour the whole of the Stalinallee workforce had joined in. Fifteen hundred workers headed for the Alexanderplatz and the seats of East German government. By the time they got there the leaders had 3000 marching men behind them. The police, certainly wisely and perhaps sympathetically, held the traffic lights at green for them.

From the Alexanderplatz they headed towards the East German government buildings in the Leipzigerstrasse, the former headquarters of Goering's Luftwaffe. On the way they were joined by more building workers who were repairing the State Opera House, and also by thousands who were not building workers at all. Between the Alexanderplatz and the Leipzigerstrasse the demonstrators started to demand not only the abolition of the decision to raise the norms but also free elections and a new government. The People's Police retired into their barracks and barred the doors.

The assembled demonstrators demanded to see Walter Ulbricht, the General Secretary of the East German Socialist Unity Party or SED and East Germany's virtual dictator, or the Prime Minister, Otto Grotewohl. Neither would show his face. Instead the crowd were given a glimpse of the Deputy Prime Minister, Heinrich Rau, and the Minister of Mines, Fritz Selbmann, peering out of a window. The crowd did not go away. Eventually, as the cries got louder and the demands for freedom and free elections became more frequent, Herr Selbmann appeared at the door of the government buildings. Someone gave him a table to stand on. Someone else called, successfully, for quiet. Selbmann, who deserved a medal of a sort, then said that the norms would not be raised. The crowd said that that was no longer enough. They wanted freedom, they said. A man got on to the table beside Selbmann. He had been in Nazi concentration camps because he believed in freedom. Was it not possible to have freedom now? If he disappeared from his workplace tomorrow his comrades would know that he had been sent back to the prison that Hitler had sent him to. The demonstrators meant what they said about freedom. The call went out for a general strike to be held the next day, Wednesday, 17 June.

The Red Army arrived in the night. By dawn at least ten type T34 tanks were stationed outside the government buildings in the Leipzigerstrasse and more were seen outside other government buildings in the Wilhelmstrasse. Large contingents of Soviet infantry appeared near the Brandenburg Gate and the Potsdamerplatz, both on the border between the British and Soviet sectors. The People's Police, who had also emerged from their barracks during the night, were out in force and armed. There were unconfirmed reports of a railway strike in the Soviet zone and of further unrest in Leipzig, Gera, Bitterfeld, Halle, and Torgau. At half past one in the afternoon the Soviet military administration declared a state of emergency in East Berlin.

Wednesday was worse than Tuesday. Instead of 3000 demonstrators in the Leipzigerstrasse there were 10,000 by early morning. This time the police and the Red Army opened fire. By the evening there were at least seven dead, six shot by the police, one run down and killed by a Russian tank. The main conflicts flared up at three places – the Brandenburg Gate, the Potsdamerplatz, and the Friedrichstrasse. In spite of the fire power arrayed against them the demonstrators raised hell everywhere. They climbed the Brandenburg Gate. They tore down the Red Flag which usually flies there, and set fire to it. They took over the Soviet bookshop and set fire to that too. They disabled at least two tanks by putting baulks of wood through their tracks and into the muzzles of their guns. They drove the People's Police out of a district headquarters in the Columbia House on the Potsdamerplatz and then set fire to the empty building.

During the day the Berlin demonstrators were joined by steelworkers from the Soviet zone steel plant of Hennigsdorf which lies to the west of Berlin. The steelworkers marched through the French sector of Berlin to join the East Berlin demonstrators.

Thursday was the day of retribution. In declaring a state of emergency the previous day the Soviet Military Commandant, Major General Dibrowa, had forbidden 'all demonstrations, gatherings, and congregations of more than three people'. His declaration said that if these were to take place in public those who took part in them would be punished according to military law. He also imposed a curfew from 9 p.m. until 5 o'clock in the morning. On the Thursday East Berlin was calm and deserted, though the courts were not. As a first step the Soviet military authorities tried and found guilty of 'provocation in the service of a foreign intelligence agency' a thirty-five-year-old unemployed West Berliner called Willi Göttling. He was condemned to death and shot immediately. Meanwhile on the Stalinallee where it had all begun, Soviet tanks were still in position, Soviet infantrymen on patrol. So were People's Policemen in large groups. The Soviet tanks could point their guns in whichever direction they wanted, but the bricklayers stayed idle, as did the carpenters, the plumbers, and all the building workers in sight.

At this time more reports began to reach Berlin about parallel uprisings in the Soviet zone itself. A state of emergency had been declared in Potsdam, Babelsberg, and Chemnitz. Strikes and demonstrations were reported from Brandenburg, Dresden, Halle, Leipzig, Erfurt, Cottbus, Rostock, Warnemünde, and Magdeburg, where twenty people were reported shot dead by the Russian army. These reports suggested that virtually the whole of the Soviet zone of occupation (or of the German Democratic Republic) had been affected by the events in East Berlin. The reports could not be confirmed at the time – there was no question of Western reporters being allowed to investigate these places – and could not readily be confirmed until some time afterwards, but a painstaking collection of charges, verdicts, and sentences, available in the Ullstein Archiv in West Berlin, shows that Willi Göttling was not the only one to be shot, although he was probably the first. Generally speaking sentences of death were passed and executed by the Soviet authorities and prison sentences by the German ones. In Magdeburg, also on the Thursday, a Soviet military court sentenced Alfred Ardetsch and Herbert Strauch to death for taking part in demonstrations. Peter Heider, Walter Schädlich, and Heinz Sonntag were sentenced to death in Leipzig, also by Soviet military courts. Alfred Diener was sentenced to death by a Soviet court in Gera, Günther Schwarzer and Axel Schäfer by a Soviet military court in Erfurt, but not until the following week. Erna Dorn was sentenced to death in Halle on 22 June, but, exceptionally, by a German court. A week later, on 30 June, Heinz Brandt and Vera Knoblauch were sentenced to death by a Soviet court in Rostock. So was an East German coastguard, Ernst Markgraf, along with another coastguard, Hans Wojkowsky.

The German courts were slower than the Soviet ones; at the same time, they dealt with many more cases. According to the best estimates now available, about four hundred persons were convicted and sentenced to terms of imprisonment up to life and down to two years' hard labour. The Soviet courts stepped in first in order to make an example, and probably also because the German courts were impeded by an unfortunate (from the East German government's point of view) change of direction at the Ministry of Justice. The Minister, Max Fechner, a toolmaker and a former Social Democrat who had been swept into the Socialist Unity Party, was unwise enough to say publicly that the right to strike was enshrined in the East German constitution. And he was quite right. The right to strike *is* proclaimed loudly.

Proclamations are one thing, but the realities of dictatorship another. Having foolishly quoted the Constitution on 1 July, Herr Fechner was quickly arrested and sent to a concentration camp – probably to Sachsenhausen, which had conveniently been left intact by Hitler. Fechner's successor, Hilde Benjamin, was not concerned about what the Constitution said about the right to strike. The East German courts then went ahead.

There is a good deal of evidence for the theory that the East German government's decision to raise the norms was the result of economic problems which they could not solve, of confusion and, in the end, a degree of panic. 1953 was the year of Stalin's death. After this event (he died on 5 March) the Soviet government reviewed its policies, including its policy towards East Germany. The powerful and intelligent political adviser to the Soviet Control Commission in East Germany, Vladimir Semeonov, was recalled to Moscow on 22 April for new instructions and returned to Berlin on 5 June. Simultaneously the Soviet Control Commission was dissolved and replaced by a High Commission of which Semeonov was the Chairman. Most of the evidence suggests that his instructions were to tell the East German authorities that they must become independent economically. The Soviet Union wanted to keep more consumer goods for its own people and for other satellites. The East Germans would have to tighten their belts or make their economy more efficient or both. If these were the instructions that Semeonov brought back with him from Moscow, they would certainly be consistent with Khrushchev's known desire – as Stalin's successor – to reduce austerity at home.

In any case the East German government seems to have been greatly perplexed during the early part of June 1953. Prices were rising in the state shops. The pressure to have wages keep up with them was strong. But there is no sure way of knowing how the decision to raise the norms came about. As the Polish government has since discovered, it is possible to persuade the workers to agree with you on a great many matters but not when it comes to accepting a cut in their standard of living. Ten per cent more bricks laid for the same money means less money for the same amount of work. Whichever way the government put the proposition the workers could understand the truth behind it. The East Germans are not stupid. Nor, for that matter, was the Socialist Unity Party newspaper, *Neues Deutschland*, which – the week before the uprising – printed a prominent article saying that the norms should not be raised, or would not be raised, without the consent of the workers themselves. The workers probably did not need to be told by *Neues Deutschland* that they were being sold down the river. But it is to the paper's credit that the article appeared.

At 10.36 on the evening of 17 June the West Berlin City Council met to debate, hopelessly, the events in the East. Even while the deputies were at work the death toll among East Berliners rose from one dead and sixty wounded to ten dead and sixty-six wounded. Leaders of all parties expressed their horror and dismay. But virtually the only measure they could think of which might help the East Berliners was to provide them with abundant medical aid.

June the Seventeenth, as the Berliners call it, demonstrated three truths which may or may not be eternal. The first is that even the harshest and best-organized dictatorship cannot lightly or easily order a reduction in the standard of living of its subjects. The strike weapon is effective everywhere, even in East Berlin. You cannot accomplish everything with guns. The second truth established in 1953 is that even then, eight years after the end of World War II, the Soviet authorities in East Germany were in effective charge. It was the Soviet military courts, not the East German ones, which convened at once to sentence Germans to death. It was the Red Army, not the East German one, which occupied the Potsdamerplatz and the Stalinallee.

The third truth is that, at that tragic moment in Berlin's history, the resisters were not Berliners only. The whole of the Soviet zone was equally disturbed and militant. I hope very much that the man from Rostock whom I met in the Stalinallee on 17 June was not one of those condemned to death on 18 June. But he was there, and so were many others from well outside Berlin.

17 June served only to reinforce the West Berliners' conviction that compromise with the East German government was out of the question. You cannot parley with people who shoot strikers dead. Until the week of the uprising there still were friends of mine in West Berlin who believed that reunification of the city would be possible. From then on they changed their minds. Kinship still united the Berliners to the extent that families could get together even if parts of the family lived on the other side of the border. West Berlin children could still visit their grandparents in Pankow. East Berlin children could visit Charlottenburg. But the border was there, and to the east of it human rights were in question, or at least they did not conform to the standards that the West Berliners had come to expect. Having been deprived of democracy for so long by Hitler, West Berlin set for itself some high democratic standards. In those days – though not always subsequently – no West Berlin politician could pull the wool over anybody's eyes. The Schoeneberger Rathaus was the seat of what may well have been the cleanest government in Europe.

It was also a government which presided over the most remarkable component of the German economic miracle. West Berlin, largely rebuilt, proceeded to pull itself up by its bootstraps. The West Berliners' ingenuity, their diligence, and their fortitude were all harnessed to a mighty attempt to earn an honest living in a cold and competitive world.

The attempt was heroic. West Berlin since the war has had to reckon with the fact that its markets in the West are far away, its raw material supplies can only be expensive, and it has no room to expand. There can hardly have been a less favourable situation when it came to economic geography. It was as if a lighthouse-keeper were trying to earn a living by running a machine-shop. This, roughly speaking, is what the West Berliners did. They put their expertise to the best possible use. They made it their business to explore the markets for specialized products whose manufacture required much skill but not much in the way of raw materials. They were supported loyally by the West German Republic and by the Deutschemark. Everyone knows that Bonn subsidizes Berlin, but this does not mean that the West Berliners enjoy the status of pensioners. They have never taken their ease in the conviction that West Germany will always pay.

West Berlin prospered. East Berlin did not. The prosperity gap widened through the 1960s. The most obvious result was a flood of refugees anxious to better themselves from East to West. Until 1961 it still was possible for Berliners to cross the Iron Curtain and take up jobs, prosperity and residence in the West.

For eight years after 17 June the two standards of living drew apart. So did the two currencies. The East German authorities would only allow West Berliners to change their Deutschemarks for Eastern ones at an exchange rate of one for one. Everybody knew that this was ridiculous. The black market rate was one Deutschemark for four or five Eastern ones. No one even tried to pretend that the East German authorities were doing anything else but protect their currency as best they could.

What they could not protect, however, was their people. As the grass grew greener in West Berlin and Western Germany, more and more East Germans and East Berliners emigrated to the West. In the end the East German authorities decided to risk the obloquy and to lock them in.

13
A Wall to Keep People In

One hour before dawn on 14 August 1961, the North Atlantic Treaty Organization asked Corporal Michael Moore of 'C' Squadton the 4th Royal Tank Regiment, what he could see in front of him. Corporal Moore and his men were NATO's spearhead. They were the crew of the only tank that the Western world could deploy in the Invalidenstrasse on the boundary between the British and the Soviet sectors of Berlin.

What was happening was that the East Germans, powerfully supported by the Russians, were building a wall through Berlin to prevent the East Germans from escaping to the West. The Invalidenstrasse, which is narrow, was also a key crossing point between East and West Berlin, and crosses the border at the Sandkrug bridge. NATO asked Corporal Moore what he could see because NATO needed to know. Corporal Moore, with the patience of the Commander at the sharp end of the problem, said that he could see nothing because it was too dark. 'Every now and again I would search around visually, using the episcopes and binoculars, but if the image is black, magnifying black seven times over doesn't really improve it.'

Corporal Moore knew that he was the sharp end of NATO.

Every half-hour I was called to say could I see anything, did I hear anything, could I guess what was going on. And I couldn't. And then about 4 a.m. it got a little bit lighter. You could just sense the sun beginning to come up. So I had another look. And then things began to take some sort of shape...

As the light came up slowly, it started to identify. Sure enough it was a tank and I was asked what sort of a tank. It was a Soviet tank. These were the questions coming from them. 'What sort of tank?' 'Wait a minute. It's got tracks and a gun but just give me time till the light comes up.' When the light came up I said, 'It's a T34–85.' Eventually I spotted the marker-plate on the side and I said, 'Yes, it's a Soviet tank, it is a T34–85 and it is definitely Soviet.' They wanted to know how far away it was and I said, 'It's about 15 metres.' To which they replied, 'Did you say 15 metres?' I said, 'Yes I did.'

I could only assume that the Soviet tank had been there when I arrived at a quarter to twelve and that he must have heard me moving into position. But, of course, I didn't then know that he was there. So perhaps he had an advantage in that respect. When daylight came up for real the distance was 15 metres and that was really from tank-hull to tank-hull. So our gun-barrels were more or less 5 metres apart, the end of my gun-barrel to the end of his. So what do you do in a situation like that?

Being all good Brits anyway, in times of crisis, what we always do is to have a cup of tea. Tankies are no different from each other. When you have been sitting there all night you're dying for a cup of tea and, of course, my radio operator-loader, who also is the sort of chef aboard a tank, had already brewed the tea, had got the egg sandwiches ready and produced for me my mug of tea and sandwich for breakfast which I used to accept as my right as a governor on the tank. I propped it up on the front of my hatch as usual and started to drink my tea.

Till then there had been no sign of life from the T34. It could have been an empty hull. But then – and I nearly spilled my tea at this stage – the commander's hatch on the Russian tank opened and a head appeared wearing one of those super Soviet helmets that they seem to have and a pair of binoculars and all I could see was a head and binoculars and him looking at me and me looking at him. I suppose he was probably intrigued about the tea more than anything else. One thing we could establish is that there was no way that he was going to have a cup of tea or coffee because they had no facilities in their tanks for brewing at all.

I looked at him again and got no response at all. I finished my tea and moved up a little bit in the turret and he did so as well. So, then I thought, in for a penny, in for a pound. I just gave him a gentle wave, nothing else. I got no reaction at all other than his disappearing out of sight and the lid closing rapidly. Whether I had upset him or whether his manual didn't cover exchanges of greetings with tankmen of the British Army – I don't know.

The building of the wall was the Berliners' ultimate trauma. It was as if Times Square in New York had been bisected, or a frontier erected in the Strand in London. The wall permitted no compromise. You could not cross it without permission, and if you had no permission there were men with guns who would shoot you. Psychologically as well as physically it was an appalling blow to a community which had been an entity since the twelfth century.

The Western Allies did their best to cheer people up. After confronting the Warsaw Pact in the Invalidenstrasse on NATO's behalf, Corporal Moore was sent out to encourage the West Berliners.

I suppose it would be sort of showing ourselves, showing the British might, as it was, and our six tanks really kept occupying various positions along the British sector. I spent the next six weeks, just about every night, following the progress of the wall and looking at its building. In about three months, I think it was, one really could see the change in the attitude of the Berliners. We had seen a position where Berlin was an open city. We had seen then, suddenly, the position where it was a divided city and we had seen the shock to the inhabitants of this city. After that we were getting evidence of the readjustment of the Berliners.

We went on a tour of the British sector with our tanks, and this was about, say, four or five months after the building of the wall. One never realized until that time how much one was appreciated by the citizens of Berlin. I am not old enough to have been in the Normandy landings or the occupation of the great cities throughout Europe, but having seen films of it, I was rather reminded of those days. My tank drove through West Berlin down the Kurfuerstendamm. It ended up covered in flowers. People were throwing flowers at us. They were giving us gifts. Bottles of beer and every sort of gift right through the city. They were lining the road, three and four deep. They were cheering and shouting and one wondered at the time why there was this great fuss over nothing.

In the best traditions of Hitler's blitzkriegs, the East Germans began to build their wall between midnight and dawn on a Sunday. The first indication that something was up was when the East Germans stopped a train. It was the 0110 from Staaken to West Berlin. The passengers were told to get out, given their money back, and told that the train would not run. Staaken is the border station on the S-Bahn between the British sector and the Soviet zone. The S-Bahn is the Soviet-controlled elevated railway. The train retired without explanation, westward into the zone.

The duty police commissioner for West Berlin heard about this at 1.54 a.m. from the police in Spandau. One minute later, at 1.55, the police section commander in Wedding reported that S-Bahn traffic at the Gesundbrunnen had been stopped altogether. Gesundbrunnen is nowhere near the border with the Soviet zone but it is quite close to the border between the West Berlin borough of Wedding and the East German borough of Prenzlauer Berg. It is an important junction controlling four lines on the S-Bahn – a kind of Earls Court of North Berlin. The commissioner decided that the second stoppage was not a coincidence, that something was up, and that he had better wake his chief constable. At 2.15 a.m. the chief constable, Erich Duensing, ordered a general alert and informed the Allied authorities in the three Western sectors.

The police were right. At 2.30 a.m. on what was now Sunday, 13 August, the police patrol at the Brandenburg Gate reported that twenty-three personnel carriers carrying People's Policemen had occupied the Pariserplatz which lies just to the east of the Gate and that they had also stopped all traffic passing through the Gate. There was more of the same. Until at five minutes past three, again from the neighbourhood of Spandau, another police report came in saying that a strong force of tanks and Russian soldiers had been seen on Federal Highway 5, a main road leading out of Berlin in a westerly direction and which turns into the Heerstrasse when it crosses the city boundary. The first real clue to what was up came five minutes later. The Ebertstrasse, which runs south from the Brandenburg Gate to the Potsdamerplatz and which virtually forms the boundary between the British and Soviet zones, was being torn up by squads of labourers. Half a mile north they were laying barbed wire in the Bernauerstrasse – a particularly sensitive part of the frontier because it ends at the front doors of the residents' houses.

As the morning wore on it became clear why the East Germans were tearing up the roads. They were preparing first to lay obstacles like barbed wire and, behind them, to build on territory belonging to the Soviet sector the wall which is still there today.

As the news got round that Berlin was being divided by a wall Berliners flocked to watch and some of them to protest. The People's Police had been expecting this. Their job, it became evident, was to protect the building workers who were tearing up the roads and building the wall itself. The Berliners came from both sides of the border. By late afternoon about four thousand West Berliners had arrived in the Bernauerstrasse to watch, jeer, and complain. About ten thousand had gathered on the western side of the Brandenburg Gate. By nightfall the People's Police had sent for water cannon in case of trouble.

Fortification of the wall continued through the autumn. By the end of November the sectors opposite the Brandenburg Gate and the Potsdamerplatz had been made secure against attack by tanks. By then the two parts of the city had been almost completely severed. Only 500 West Berliners had been given visas to visit their city's eastern half. On 18 November, the last of 1300 children under five, who had happened to be spending the week-end during which the wall was built with relatives on the wrong side of the border, were restored to their parents by the German Red Cross. The elevated and underground railways no longer connected the two parts of the town. There was no direct telephone communication. Only the mails were left. An eight-coach mail train commuted each night between East and West Berlin. Sometimes it had to be supplemented by lorry loads of letters and parcels, solemnly exchanged at a bridge in the Heinrich Heinestrasse.

Four other crossing points were still available to West Berliners. Everywhere else the wall was impenetrable. It followed the eastern boundaries of five of Berlin's boroughs, Reinickendorf, Wedding, Tiergarten, Kreuzberg, and Neukölln. Within the city itself the wall was then 26½ miles long, starting in the north, at the junction of the French sector with the Soviet zone and the Soviet sector.

The wall starts in a bird sanctuary on the banks of a stream called the Tegelerfliess. This flows through a marshy valley two hundred yards from the village of Lübars, which has four big farms, a policeman, a duckpond and an inn called the 'Merry Finch'. The village is reputed to be the coldest place in Berlin. It belongs to the French sector of the city and the high road leading out of it leads only to the Russian sector. The barrier is seven minutes from the 'Merry Finch' but the East German People's Police can see you sooner. Here, as everywhere along the wall, they operate in pairs, one man with the field-glasses, the other with the gun.

At this point and by November 1961, the barrier consisted of three barbed-wire fences supported on concrete posts seven feet high and six inches thick. The first fence was and still is on the border itself: the second is ten feet behind the first: the third is 150 yards behind the second. Each fence had up to ten strands of barbed wire and the ground between the first and second was obstructed with more barbed wire coiled over wooden supports consisting of two crosses linked together and resembling, but for the wire, gigantic devices for keeping carving-knives off tablecloths.

The ground between the second and third fences had been cleared and could be lit at night. A line of poles thirty feet high, spaced thirty yards apart, carried a power line; each pole had a cluster of electric lights. There was, already then, a line of watchtowers twenty feet high, spaced six hundred yards apart.

Further south, where the suburbs become denser, the border is marked by a railway embankment. In Berlin, as in Surrey, railway lines in leafy suburbs tend to be flanked by gardens. The People's Police had managed to get rid of most of the gardens that were in their way on the east side of the track. They burned the rubbish, the tool sheds along with the cherry trees, at the Bornholmerstrasse station.

About a mile further south is the Bernauerstrasse in the borough of Wedding. At this point the sector boundary runs east and west and coincides with the building line on the south side of the street. Here, as in other places, the East Germans have made their wall out of houses. At first they bricked up the front doors and the ground-floor windows. Later they blocked up all the windows; people who lived on the south side of the street in the Soviet sector were talking illegally to people who lived on the north side.

Some of them were doing more than that. At a bus stop opposite No. 44 neighbours have put up a cross in memory of a student called Bernd Lünser, who, pursued by the People's Police, jumped off the roof on 4 October 1961. The West Berlin Fire Department tried, but failed, to catch him in a jumping-sheet. Bernd Lünser risked much to get out. No. 44 is five storeys high.

Two hundred yards down the road from No. 44 is the grave-yard of the Church of the Atonement, Wedding. Further west again is the graveyard of the Church of St Sophia. There is also the French cemetery in the Liesenstrasse. The wall runs through all three.

Round the corner is the Invalidenstrasse crossing point. For a long time, a poster across the road said bleakly: 'The stronger the German Democratic Republic gets the greater is the certainty of peace in Germany.' It was here that an East German railway policeman shot and killed an unknown man who had dived into the neighbouring Humboldt Dock from the grounds of the Charité Hospital. From the Humboldt Dock the wall follows the bank of the Spree to skirt the Reichstag building and on to the Branden-burg Gate.

When they first fortified the Gate the East Germans began by sinking a row of steel posts into the roadway and cementing them in. They then laid slotted prefabricated concrete slabs over the posts which projected through the slabs and held them steady. They then poured wet cement over the slabs and laid another layer on top, repeating the process until they had made a multi-decker sandwich seven feet high and six feet thick, a sandwich in which slabs of concrete had been substituted for bread, and wet cement for butter.

The wall follows to the inch the western boundary of East Berlin which, in front of the Gate, bulges out into the roadway in a segment of a circle one hundred yards wide and fifty deep. It took the East German construction workers fifty-three hours to finish the job. They were heavily guarded by People's Police. For three days they ate at a field kitchen parked beneath the Gate. From the Gate down the Ebertstrasse to the Potsdamerplatz they added, in the same period, two rows of heavy welded steel tripods, fixed in the roadway with cement.

From the Potsdamerplatz the wall runs south to include the ruins of the Potsdam station, then north again, then east towards the Spree. It bisects the Wilhelmstrasse immediately south of what used to be Goering's Air Ministry. The next street east is the Friedrichstrasse, where non-Germans may cross the border at a point which has come to be known as Checkpoint Charlie. It is a narrow place of tension where only one tank can operate at a time. Here, for a day and two nights in October 1961, the United States and Russia faced each other with their guns loaded. The whole might and purpose of NATO was represented by the gunner of a single Patton tank, Private Baker, aged twenty, of Michigan.

The next gap in the wall is at the Heinrich Heinestrasse. Coffins are exchanged here on Wednesdays. The wall runs thence along the northern boundary of the borough of Kreuzberg round the back of the Bethany Hospital to the banks of the river Spree. From the Spree for rather more than half a mile the border follows the Landwehrkanal, forty yards wide and a once-useful waterway. In Neukölln, the wall twists between blocks of flats, shops, houses, gardens. In two streets the boundary follows the building line, but here the situation that obtains in the Bernauerstrasse is reversed. The houses belong to the West, the pavement to the East.

Where this happens the wall has been built in the gutter. A notice at the end of one such street reads:

> Citizens of the Sebastianstrasse: We draw your attention to the fact that the pavement you use belongs to the territory of the German Democratic Republic and that the building line is the State frontier. We expect you to refrain from any provocation on this territory because otherwise we will take the security measures that are necessary.

The wall ends four miles on in Rudow, a distant, pleasant southern suburb on State Highway 179, the road that leads to the East Berlin airport. Under its local name, Waltersdorfer Chaussee, the road now ends in two rows of barbed wire and a slit-trench. The last house in West Berlin is No. 197: small, neat, and loved. What must have been No. 199 has been bulldozed away. It was, by all accounts, as neat and modest as 197. In the place where it used to stand the earth has been cleared and flattened. The cherry trees have long since been flung aside to make way for the wire.

The Berlin wall is the only major fortification in history to have been built to keep people in rather than to keep them out. The tank-trap, a trench twelve feet deep, runs for sixty-six miles. One side of the trench is vertical whereas the other slopes down at an angle of about thirty degrees from the horizontal. The vertical edge of the trench is on the side of the Western sector. Which means that it has been designed to prevent people driving lorries, cars, or any other vehicle, out of the Eastern sector and into the Western one. Had the purpose of the wall been truly defensive – as the East German government says it is – the trench would have been built the other way round with its vertical edge on the eastern side.

The East Germans have been working to improve the wall – if that is the word – continuously since 1961. It covers not only the sector boundaries between the Western sectors and the Eastern one, but also the landward boundaries of the Western sectors where they abut on to the East German Republic's territory. The total length of the wall is 165 kilometres or 102 miles – nearly twice the distance from London to Brighton. Sixty-three miles of the wall consist of multiple barbed-wire fences, and there are 253 watch-towers from which armed policemen can monitor the wall itself. The whole of the wall can be illuminated at night and the lights will go on automatically if anyone tries to cross a fence. There now are 260 separate dog-runs. These are fenced-in enclosures about four feet wide which any escaper would have to cross and which are inhabited by guard dogs running loose. Generally speaking an escaper has to grapple first with a high fence of which the top wire carries a lethal current; after that he may well have to contend with the dog-run, which consists of two fences with dogs in between; after that there is the tank-trap with a twelve-foot-high vertical wall on the side of freedom; after that an open space; after that another fence. The whole complex which, in the country, can cover an area as wide as a motorway, can be illuminated at night. In most places illumination is automatic as soon as anyone touches the first fence. The wall is guarded by about 15,000 men of the Central Border Command of the East German Army, of whom 13,000 man the wall day and night, while 2000 man the check-points and entrances through the wall between the Western sectors, East Germany and East Berlin. In the first sixteen years of the wall's existence they opened fire 1513 times on escapers or imagined escapers. They also used tear gas on 428 occasions and killed at least 54 persons while injuring 105 more. About 3000 people are thought to have been arrested while trying to get over the wall during this period.

One offensive characteristic of the wall is that it divides a community arbitrarily – a community which has been united for centuries. Another is the way in which the wall follows, mindlessly and without regard to the civilized realities, municipal boundaries that were laid down or came into being in the eighteenth century. There is a verdant island close to Potsdam which lies between the Wannsee and the Havel and most of which belongs to West Berlin. A minute enclave, however, belongs to Babelsberg, which in turn belongs to the East. The wall goes round it. And because the country is wooded it is, here, especially wide – an empty, irregular scar surrounding an innocent village and eating up the villagers' gardens. The same pattern defiles the countryside around another enclave further north at Eis Keller at the north-western extremity of the Spandau forest. Daily throughout the summer the East Germans harrow the open ground between the deadly fences and spray it with weedkiller. Their purpose is to ensure that the generally unfertile ground of the Mark of Branden-burg does not produce cover which could help anyone escape.

In the city itself where the wall divides the Eastern sector from the Western ones, the strip of open ground which provides the East German Army with its opportunity to shoot escapers dead is, perforce, often narrower than on the border between the Western sectors and the Soviet zone. But the spectacle is no less brutal. In the Bernauerstrasse, where the sector boundary coincides with the front walls and doors of the houses on the Eastern side, the wall has now been reconstructed to run through the porch of the Church of Atonement. The church's western porch offended the East German authorities because it extended into Western territory. The wall now runs through the back of the porch, cutting it off from the belfry and the tower. Worshippers at the Church of Atonement must find another way in. The west door is barred to them by concrete.

The wall divides into two, twenty-six Protestant and five Catholic parishes and separates thirteen parishes from their burial grounds. It has also interrupted the elevated railway service which used to run straight through from East Berlin through the Western sectors to the Soviet zone in the west and to Potsdam. Barges which used to run through West Berlin on their way to Western Germany have now been diverted through a canal thirty-five kilometres long. Above all, perhaps, the wall has altered the population flows. Previously East Berlin was a declining popula-tion whereas West Berlin was a growing one, largely because of the arrival of refugees. This has now been stopped.

On the Sunday on which the foundations of the wall were laid democratic Berlin did not sit on its hands. By now the governing Mayor was Willy Brandt. He summoned the Senate at 9.15 that

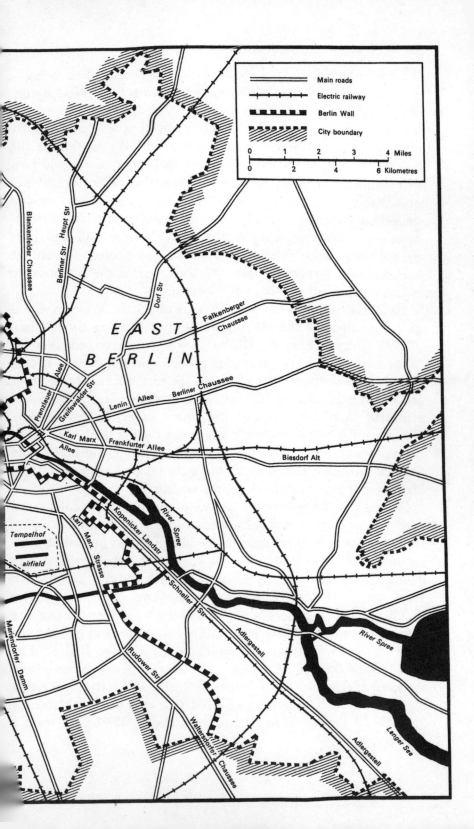

Main roads

Electric railway

Berlin Wall

City boundary

0   1   2   3   4 Miles

0   2   4   6 Kilometres

Blankenfelder Chaussee

Berliner Str   Haupt Str

Dorf Str

EAST

BERLIN

Falkenberger Chaussee

Prenzlauer Allee

Greifswalder Str

Lenin Allee

Berliner Chaussee

Karl Marx Allee

Frankfurter Allee

Biesdorf Alt

Karl Marx Strasse

Kopenicker Landstr

River Spree

Tempelhof airfield

Schneller Str

Adlergestell

River Spree

Mariendorfer Damm

Rudower Str

Waltersdorfer Chaussee

Adlergestell

Langer See

Sunday morning of 13 August 1961, the Senate then being – as it is now – the democratically chosen executive for West Berlin. The Deputy Speaker of the City Council (the speaker was on holiday) summoned a Council meeting for 6.34 the same Sunday evening. Deputy Speaker Müllerburg said: 'We hope that the holding of this extraordinary meeting will show the world how extraordinarily seriously we view the situation. The Council will presumably want to protest at the way in which these new and unjust measures have surrounded German citizens on Soviet-occupied territory with an impenetrable prison wall and have welded their chains more securely. We also protest against the harmful consequences for our city and against the intention to make permanent the division of Germany.'

As a mark of their special concern the three Western Commandants attended the meeting instead of sending their liaison officers. Deputy Speaker Müllerburg welcomed them, saying: 'Your presence at this meeting proves the seriousness of the matters we have to discuss and also the true alliance between us and our Western friends.' There were greetings and messages of sympathy from the provincial parliament at Schleswig-Holstein. There was the proud discovery that, even during the height of the holiday season and at 6.34 on a Sunday evening, the Berlin City Council had still managed to raise a quorum at short notice. Then Herr Brandt gave his report on the situation.

He said that the wall was a towering injustice. It was not just a new state frontier, it was the outer wall of a concentration camp. 'With the world as its witness the Senate of Berlin protests against an unjust and inhuman measure adopted by those who would divide Germany, who oppress East Berlin and who threaten West Berlin.' Having reported on the events of the night Herr Brandt said: 'The concrete piles which now cut through our city have been driven into the heart of German unity and through the heart of the living organism which is the City of Berlin.' The decisions and decrees of the East German regime drew breath from the spirit of falsehood and injustice. 'In the last forty-eight hours the communist regime has confessed that it is itself to blame for the flight of Germans to Germany. A clique which calls itself a government has been forced to try to imprison its own people. The concrete piles, the barbed wire, the cleared fields of fire, the watchtowers and the sub-machine guns are the characteristics of the concentration camp.'

But, sadly, Herr Brandt had to admit that the wall had done its work, that the concentration camp which now was East Germany had become an effective prison. Between noon on the Saturday and 10 a.m. on the Sunday 3190 refugees had reached West Berlin. This rate of flow of refugees – about 145 per hour – was not abnormal for a weekend before the wall was built. But from ten o'clock on the Sunday morning, Herr Brandt said, the rate had slowed down. Only 800 refugees had arrived between 10 a.m. and 4 p.m. Fifty an hour instead of 145, and at a time when the wall itself was still incomplete and even the East German authorities were still confused.

The building of the wall was, of course, the worst possible advertisement for the East German regime. Not even Walter Ulbricht, the virtual dictator of the German Democratic Republic – as East Germany had by then named itself – tried very hard to disguise the reason for building it.

The sad fact for Ulbricht was that the workers were leaving the workers' State. In the week before the wall went up about a thousand East German citizens daily were leaving East Berlin for the West. On the whole they were not dissidents like Sakharov or Solzhenitsyn. Most of them were workers and peasants whose loyalty to the communist cause has always been assumed by communist leaders. No one will ever know how many of the 1000 emigrants a day were fleeing from oppression and how many because of hard times. But there can be no doubt that in 1961 times were hard in Eastern Germany.

This was largely the result of an attempt by the East German communists – an attempt which eventually succeeded – to raise the standard of living in East Germany to higher levels than those prevailing in other East European countries. The stated aim of the 5th Congress of the Socialist Unity Party in July 1958 had been to raise East German living standards to the same level as those in Western Germany. Agriculture was to be collectivized.

There was to be a seven-year economic plan. Industrial output was to be increased but – in the interval before living standards rose – everyone would have to tighten their belts.

Not everyone wanted to do this. One hundred and forty-four thousand East Germans emigrated to the West in 1959, nearly all of them through West Berlin. In 1960 the total of emigrants had risen to 199,000. By the beginning of August 1961 the rate had risen again to 365,000 a year. Many of the emigrants were farmers who expected, with reason, that their land would be taken from them and collectivized. Others were professional people, engineers and doctors. But the great mass consisted of those industrial workers who were supposed to be the Socialist Unity Party's main base and in whose name the party claimed to govern the German Democratic Republic. The rising tide of emigration meant that East Germany was bleeding. Its most important economic asset, the skilled workers, farmers and engineers, were voting with their feet in favour of West German society and against the Seven Year Plan, the Socialist Unity Party, and Herr Ulbricht.

Ulbricht first tried to staunch the wound by persuading the Russians to take over West Berlin. He asked Khrushchev, the ruler of Russia since the death of Stalin in 1953, to lay claim forcefully to West Berlin. For if West Berlin became part of the German Democratic Republic Ulbricht could prevent the emigrants from leaving. At first Khrushchev agreed. Four months after the adoption of the Seven Year Plan, and as the stream of emigrants began to swell, Khrushchev declared in what he hoped was an ominous way that the Western powers 'no longer have any legal, moral or political basis for their continued occupation of West Berlin'. He said that the whole of Berlin belonged to the German Democratic Republic. He gave the Western powers an ultimatum. They must leave West Berlin and demilitarize it within six months from November 1958.

The Western powers paid no attention. The ultimatum ran out in May 1959, and nothing happened. Khrushchev sat on his hands. If he had meant to make a threat it was an empty one. Ulbricht's protector had let him down.

After two years during which the flow of emigrants continued to

The wall snakes round the Brandenburg Gate

The wall being built round the Reichstag

The Wall runs through the graveyard of the Church of the Atonement in the Bernauerstrasse, Wedding

Berliners welcome
President Kennedy in 1963

Left to right:
Chancellor Adenauer,
Lucius Clay (with
raised hand), President
Kennedy, Willy Brandt

grow, Ulbricht again approached the Russians. He said he would have to build the wall. The Russians agreed. The wall was built. Ulbricht's humiliation was plain for all to see.

The evidence for Ulbricht's failure was a rampart dividing a 700-year-old community into two.

17 June 1953 and 13 August 1961 were the East German government's darkest days. The world could see that the East German workers (not by any means the East German middle classes alone) were sufficiently discontented to risk their lives in protest on the first occasion, and on the second to be so anxious to leave the country that they had to be stopped. But to assume that if the wall were dismantled tomorrow, the flow of refugees or emigrants would start again at the same rate as in 1963 would be to ignore what has happened since in the German Democratic Republic.

Protected by the wall the Seven Year Plan got into its stride, although some of its footsteps faltered a little. The people, having been compelled to stay, stayed to work and to work diligently. It could be argued that the East Germans had nothing else to do in what had become their national prison. At the same time work became their vocation and economic recovery their impressive achievement. By 1974, according to a World Bank report, the annual per capita income in the German Democratic Republic was $3710 compared to annual per capita income in Britain of $3590. The individual output of East German workers put their country into eighth place among the world's industrial nations.

No one can be sure why the East Germans did this, but it is reasonable to assume that, having been hemmed in by the wall and by similar fortifications along the borders with Western Germany, they settled down to make the best of a bad job. It is also reasonable to assume that – as the West German example has shown – Germans regard personal industry and diligence as one of the highest virtues. Since 1961 the East Germans have been building their own wealth, their own homes, and in a singular way their own society. People become proud of what they have created, even if, in their hearts of hearts, they would have preferred to create something else.

What is more, by 1970, about two-thirds of the East German population had grown up since the war (they first went to school in 1945 or 1946) and had known no regime other than Hitler's when they were very small followed by Soviet military government and the German Democratic Republic. To a large extent they have done what comes naturally to Germans. They have taken to sport and athletics, scoring amazing successes at the Olympic Games. They have accepted a highly vocational educational system because they know no other. They have accepted standards of housing for the young and for the very old, which, though cheap to rent, are generally inferior to those that they could have in the West. And the whole population has accepted – or has had to accept – a sharply restricted freedom of choice. They cannot travel westwards at will because, unless they get permission, the wall will stop them. There is less choice of goods in the shops than in the West. There is no choice at all between different sets of politicians. The German Democratic Republic is governed by the Politburo of the Socialist Unity Party and the East German Parliament is a joke. Ulbricht's successor, Erich Honecker, is a virtual dictator.

It is true that he has allowed more people to visit West Germany and more West Germans to visit the Democratic Republic. Under the agreements negotiated between the two Germanies more people now move between East and West. But visas are compulsory. Freedom to move and particularly freedom to move westward, is till subject to government permission. My colleague Jonathan Steele in his definitive book on East Germany, *Socialism with a German Face*, says that: 'besides old-age pensioners, East Germans with relatives in the West can visit them for weddings, funerals and serious illness, but even in these categories young East Germans rarely get permission, and married couples cannot go together . . . The number of independent young travellers is probably small, but interest in travel remains very high in the German Democratic Republic. The lack of opportunities for it is perhaps the single most important grievance which young East Germans have. East Germans often say that if the wall were taken down for good, they would want to visit the West just to taste the forbidden fruit. But they would return. Unemployment, inflation and the economic crisis in the West have taken the glitter away.' But as Steele goes on to say, the removal of the wall is an experiment which is not going to take place. The East German authorities still are frightened that visitors to the West might become residents in the West. The German Democratic Republic may, as Mr Honecker claims, be a place of contentment which few people would want to leave. On the other hand he continues to reinforce the wall.

14
The Rough Road to Helsinki

The end of the blockade in 1949 left the Soviet Union and the Western powers more distrustful of each other than at any time since the end of World War II. The Western powers had been shaken but not dismayed by the siege of Berlin. The Russians had been taken aback by the Western powers' joint determination – particularly that of Britain and the United States – to resist Soviet pressure on Berlin. For Berlin itself the consequence was nearly two and a half decades of insecurity.

As Murphy had predicted in May 1949, the success of the airlift had proved nothing more than that the Western Allies were capable of supplying 2·1 million people by air. The agreement which brought the blockade to an end had done nothing to secure or legitimize West Berlin's future in any formal or diplomatic sense. The result was more than two decades of angry, though generally harmless bickering, usually about access to the West.

The Soviet Union and the Western Allies argued above the Berliners' heads until, at last, they concluded a four-power agreement in 1972. This secured West Berlin's position as a city under the control of the Western Allies, linked to West Germany but in no way part of it. The agreement, finally signed on 3 June 1972, guaranteed and improved communications with West Berlin and said that its ties with West Germany would be 'maintained and developed, taking into account that these Western sectors continue not to be a constituent part of the Federal Republic of Germany and not to be governed by it'. Although this part of the agreement disappointed many Berliners, it was the best bargain that they could have expected. Its merit was that it calmed the Soviet government's fears. In a speech to the 25th Congress of the Soviet Communist Party in February 1976, Brezhnev expressed his satisfaction and, indeed, his relief:

> The settlement with regard to West Berlin was one of the
> complicated questions. It will be recalled that crises upsetting
> the situation in Europe erupted over that city. But the four-
> power agreement concluded in the autumn of 1971 [and
> signed and ratified in 1972], compounded by agreements
> and understandings reached on a number of issues by the
> governments of the German Democratic Republic and the
> Federal Republic of Germany and the West Berlin Senate
> have essentially relieved the tension. We value the co-
> operation achieved in the matter with the USA, France and
> Britain. Conditions have been created to turn West Berlin
> from a source of disputes into a constructive element of peace
> and detente. All sides must only show true respect for the
> agreements reached. Unfortunately some of their signatories
> are doing far too little in this respect. We shall insist on strict
> and complete observance of all understandings. The Soviet
> Union favours a tranquil and normal life for West Berlin.

This was a sincere – if slightly grudging – acknowledgment by
the Soviet Union that a source of trouble and tension in Central
Europe had been removed. Above all, the four-power agreement
on Berlin removed an important obstacle to the Russians' major
objective of a general European settlement of frontiers. Ever since
World War II the Soviet government's first aim in Europe has
been to safeguard the Soviet Union against another invasion from
the west. Throughout the whole period the Soviet Union has
been governed by elderly, conservative men whose most important
shared experience was Hitler's brutal invasion of their country in
1941.

Stalin did not believe British and American warnings that
Hitler's invasion was imminent. Instead he put his faith in the
Ribbentrop-Molotov Pact which made Russia and Germany
allies. His faith was misplaced. For at least three decades after that
the Kremlin was haunted by the fear that treachery could come
again, that the Germans or the Western Allies or both, would
mount another invasion. To guard against this possibility Stalin

insisted at Yalta and at Potsdam on dividing Europe into two spheres of influence, his own and that of the Western powers. The Iron Curtain was conceived at Yalta and born at Potsdam and its purpose was essentially defensive. Russia's East European satellites were to constitute the glacis – the open ground in front of the Russian fortifications which would make Russia defensible.

Soviet foreign policy has been through many changes of emphasis in other areas, some of them adventurous – first in Cuba and more lately in Africa. But in Europe the Soviet government's constant aim has been to secure the frontiers of Russia even if this meant intervening in Hungary and Czechoslovakia at the risk of alienating world opinion. This preoccupation with defence was the main cause of Russia's prolonged and dogged attempts to convene the Conference on Security and Co-operation in Europe at Helsinki. What the Russians wanted and what they achieved, was a treaty signed by thirty-five heads of government or heads of state which guaranteed the inviolability of frontiers in Europe. This meant, as far as the Russians were concerned, that thirty-five governments including that of the USA, had solemnly endorsed the frontiers agreed between Stalin, Roosevelt and Churchill at Yalta and Potsdam in 1945. The Iron Curtain had been blessed by an influential multitude.

This had been the Russians' long-term aim ever since they first conceived it in 1966. The difficulty was that a host of existing problems had to be settled first. The status of West Berlin had to be settled and agreed because no one could expect thirty-five heads of government or of state to agree to respect a status and a set of rights that were still in dispute. As long as the East German frontier remained provisional it could not be declared inviolable. As long as the German Democratic Republic remained unrecognized as a state except by its immediate neighbours in the Soviet bloc, no one could be expected to speak for East Germany at Helsinki or anywhere else in an international conference.

It was clear to the Western Allies and almost certainly to the Russians as well that for these stark but logical reasons a great deal of diplomatic spade-work would have to be done between the lifting of the blockade of Berlin in May 1949, and the signing of any agreement about co-operation and security in Europe as a whole. In the event the Helsinki Agreement was signed on 1 August 1975 – more than twenty-six years after the lifting of the blockade.

The main Soviet aim – a surrogate peace treaty which would write 'Finis' to World War II and would give Russia the feeling of security she craved – became obvious in 1966. In July of that year the Political Consultative Committee of the Warsaw Pact, meeting in Bucharest, resolved that 'it is of great positive importance to convene an all-European Conference to discuss questions of ensuring security in Europe and establishing all-European co-operation'. The Bucharest resolution also outlined the main points of what was to become the Helsinki Agreement on frontiers and their inviolability.

However, one towering Soviet initiative had diminished, almost to vanishing point, Western confidence in Soviet goodwill. This was the invasion of Dubček's liberally inclined Czechoslovakia in 1968 by Soviet, East German, and other non-Czechoslovakian East European forces. There had already been the Red Army's intervention to restore the status quo after the revolt in Hungary in 1956; Khrushchev's ultimatum to the Western powers in November 1958 which told them to get out of Berlin and which they ignored; the building of the Berlin wall in 1961; Khrushchev's adventures in Cuba which brought the world to the brink of nuclear war. And there had been two periods – in 1963 and 1965 – during which the Soviet authorities harassed British and American military traffic between West Berlin and West Germany.

The Russians had not made it easy for other Europeans, let alone the Americans, to conclude that the Soviet government's professed desire for co-operation and security in Europe was altogether sincere. In particular it was difficult for them to believe that the government whose troops had invaded Hungary and Czechoslovakia meant what it said about 'non-interference in the affairs of other states'.

Brezhnev made matters worse in the aftermath of the invasion of Czechoslovakia when he said on 13 November 1968, in a speech to the 5th Congress of the Polish Communist Party that:

> When internal and external forces hostile to socialism attempt
> to turn the development of a socialist country in the direction
> of the restoration of the capitalist system, when a threat arises
> to the cause of socialism in that country, a threat to the
> security of the Socialist Commonwealth as a whole, it
> becomes not only a problem for the people of that country
> but also a general problem, the concern of all socialist
> countries.

This, the so-called Brezhnev Doctrine, seemed to the Western
powers to negate or render dubious everything that the Soviet
government was saying about non-interference in the internal
affairs of other states. The Western statesmen proceeded, nevertheless, to prepare for Helsinki, and with Berlin in mind. But the
next move had to come from the West German Federal government in Bonn.

Under Christian Democratic Chancellors Adenauer, Erhard
and Kiesinger, the Federal Republic had refused to recognize
East Germany as a separate state. Under the so-called Hallstein
Doctrine, West Germany had refused also to recognize other states
which recognized East Germany. While the Christian Democrats
ruled, the confrontation between Bonn and East Germany was
absolute and admitted of no compromise. But once Willy Brandt
had become Chancellor – the first and last to have suffered under
Hitler, to the extent of being exiled – West Germany could admit
publicly and formally that the Germans owed a debt to the Russians
for Hitler's aggression. Brandt was qualified, as no one else could
have been, to speak to the Russians, the Poles and the Czechs
convincingly about atonement. He risked his political future in the
Federal Republic, bravely and without hesitation, for the sake
first of understanding and then of treaties with Poland and the
Soviet Union. These recognized the Oder-Neisse line as the
eastern frontier of Germany.

This was in itself a difficult decision for Brandt and also for the
Bundestag in Bonn, because it acknowledged in writing the loss
of a large area which had been German for centuries. Brandt's

final task, however, was even harder politically. His large problem was to devise, negotiate and ratify an agreement between the Federal Republic and the German Democratic Republic. The existence of such an agreement – indeed the very thought of it – implied the acceptance of the division of Germany. It was as if President Lincoln were to have concluded a treaty with the Confederates. A country which had for a century regarded itself as one nation was being asked to admit that the family had been split. Before he could ratify the treaty with Eastern Germany, Brandt had a terrible time in the Bundestag. He won in the end, though by a narrow margin. The 'Basic Treaty' between West and East Germany recognized that the two states were 'not foreign to each other'. At the same time it was a treaty between two separate governments. It was an acknowledgment of Germany's division, but it did not admit that there were two German nations.

The immediate consequence was that (the Hallstein Doctrine having been abolished) a plethora of governments recognized the East German regime. East Germany, having thus been made legitimate, entered the councils of the world. Both German states became members of the United Nations on 18 September 1973. The occupying powers had agreed to regulate the status of Berlin. Each of the two German governments had recognized the other. The road to Helsinki was open.

EPILOGUE

The Island City

The Helsinki Agreement pleased the neutrals but did little to change the attitudes of the principals. There was a great deal of brave talk on the Western side about human rights which were supposed to have been enshrined in the so-called 'Basket Three', but in fact the literal enforcement of Basket Three, which called for freedom of expression, of political association and of the right to dissent from government policy, would have meant the downfall of the Soviet government and of all its satellite governments in Eastern Europe. Brezhnev had not gone to Helsinki to sign his own political death warrant. Helsinki remained principally a restatement of existing frontiers including those which surround Berlin. For the Berliners its chief merit was that it stabilized the frontiers of their city, for thirty-five governments had signed an undertaking which said so. But the wall remained and so did the guards and their dogs. Nor could any agreement change Berlin's unhappy geographical position. There still are 211 miles between the Fulda Radio Beacon and the one in Berlin. It still only takes forty minutes to drive from Berlin to Poland. West Berlin still is a democratic outpost but a lonely one.

One of Berlin's most serious drawbacks is that it can easily be forgotten. Egon Bahr, one of Willy Brandt's closest associates, told the *New Yorker* in 1974: 'The wall was like a terrible traffic accident. The victim is taken to the hospital, operated on, wakes up after surgery, and is taken to his room, where friends are waiting. They tell him he is lucky he didn't lose his life. Then the friends go away. Eventually, the patient discovers that one of his legs has been amputated.'

West Berlin is the pleasantest city in Germany but not the richest. Many Berliners, especially the younger ones, have emigrated to West Germany where the grass is greener. West Berlin's main industry now is the staging of conferences, festivals, or major cultural events. The production of real wealth in the form of manufacture has declined simply because of distance and because the markets surrounding Berlin are closed to Berlin's exports.

In the thirty years between 1948 and 1978, Berlin has changed in character in two ways which make an obvious difference to anyone who has lived in and loved that curious city.

The young Berliners who have emigrated to the West have been replaced by Turks. Berlin now is the fourth largest Turkish city in the world. The Turkish *Gast-arbeiter* have taken over the jobs that the young West Berliners did not want to perform. They have also taken over, largely, the unlovely borough of Kreuzberg. This is neither a ghetto nor a settlement, but the Turkish population predominates. And the Turks who, in spite of an outward air of perpetual gloom, are resourceful, hard-working, and cheerful people, do not disturb Berlin life or society. They are welcome guests and important ones. West Berlin now depends upon them and would feel lost without them.

Another important, striking, and mainly wholesome fact about life in West Berlin is that it is a city without distant suburbs. Because of the wall, no one can commute to the equivalent of Long Island, Dorking, Neuilly or even Watford. The result is that central Berlin does not become deserted and go to sleep at five o'clock in the afternoon. Unlike the Barbican or Bond Street, the Kurfuerstendamm remains an animated place until late at night. The West Berliners remain a real community. They – Turks included – are a closer band of brothers and sisters than they would be if they were free to travel to the rustic delights of Potsdam and the Mark of Brandenburg.

The West Berliners do not complain overmuch about their isolation. Their links with the people who saved them in 1948 remain as strong as ever. West Berlin is and will remain a special place in the memories of all the fliers who helped to save it in 1948 and 1949. It also has a special place in the consciences of the

West European nations and of the United States. The saving of West Berlin from communist hegemony was the last great task that the British and the Americans did together. Though many British and American politicians have forgotten what was done in their name in those days, the pilots have remembered. They constitute still a brotherhood of liberators.

However, the loyalties that were forged thirty years ago cannot by themselves secure West Berlin's future. It can never be an altogether tranquil place, partly because of its isolation so crudely emphasized by the wall, but partly also because its future – like that of the rest of Europe – depends upon the nuclear deterrent. The question at the back of every thinking West Berliner's mind is whether their city is sufficiently important in the eyes of the President of the United States to warrant the threat of dropping a nuclear bomb on Moscow. From Berlin's point of view, and from the point of view of most West Europeans, the change that has taken place since 1948 which matters most to us all is that the Russians did not then have nuclear bombs but that they have them now. In April 1948, Churchill, still as belligerent as ever, suggested that the Western powers should use nuclear weapons to 'raze' the cities of Russia. No one agreed with him. Nevertheless at that time the suggestion was at least rational from the strictly military point of view. Today the destruction of Moscow would also mean, and with an awful certitude, the destruction of New York as well.

The West Berliners can comprehend as clearly as anyone else the appalling extent to which the stakes in the international power game have multiplied since the blockade. The West Berliners also realize, and probably better than most people, the extent to which the Soviet Air Force has developed its skills and capabilities. It is no longer what the American pilots used to call 'a fair weather air force' which could be relied upon not to leave the ground if the weather was bad. Nor do the Western powers still possess the immense superiority in airlift capacity that they enjoyed in 1948. Every six months the Soviet Air Force 'rotates' the Soviet garrison in Eastern Germany. That is to say, once every six months the

Soviet Air Force transfers 700,000 soldiers from the Soviet Union to East Germany and 700,000 soldiers from East Germany to the Soviet Union; and the operation takes forty-eight hours.

It does not console the West Berliners to know that their home is the pivotal point of the balance of power in Europe. The question that hangs over West Berlin more ominously than over any other city is whether the balance of power in Europe will remain undisturbed. The best guess is that it will. Soviet foreign policy in Europe, as distinct from Soviet foreign policy in other parts of the world like the Middle East, Africa, and the Far East, has not changed much. It has always been essentially defensive since the Russians gave up their attempt to blockade Berlin in May 1949. Since then there have been the intrusions into Hungary and Czechoslovakia but, objectionable though they were as attempts to interfere with the government of other countries, they did not constitute aggression against the West.

The man responsible for Soviet foreign policy for most of this time, Andrei Gromyko, is the longest-serving foreign minister in the world. He is surrounded by like-minded diplomats, most of whom he has trained himself. Failing a palace revolution in the Kremlin of even greater magnitude than the one which followed the death of Stalin, the likelihood is that the Soviet Union will continue to want stability on its western frontiers. Otherwise the Soviet government would not have signed the four-power agreement on the status of West Berlin and would certainly not have pressed over a period of decades for the signature of the Helsinki Agreement.

The Soviet government's desire for peace and stability in Western Europe, a desire which is often doubted by Western statesmen, reflects the appalling memories which haunt all the Soviet nations of the German attack on the Soviet Union in 1941. The attack was treacherous, brutal, and well-nigh disastrous for the Soviet Union. Twenty million Soviet citizens died. Millions more lost all that they had. Soviet citizens of all generations remain resentfully conscious of the consequences for their country of relying upon a treaty with the Germans. The result for the

Russians was betrayal, carnage, and a lasting suspicion of the West Europeans. Napoleon had done it before. Hitler did it again. It would be idle, even now, to expect the Russians to put all their trust in treaties with the West in Europe. From their point of view, which is more influenced by history than the point of view of the Western governments, the United States and Britain are more trustworthy partners than Germany and France. If it should ever come to a new confrontation over Berlin as grave as that of 1948 the man to whom the Russians would look first, and in whom they would first of all put their trust, would be the President of the United States of the day. 'I am a Berliner,' said President John F. Kennedy in a memorable shout uttered in the Berlin dialect. The West Berliners took this to be more than a passing incantation. The United States, Britain, and France have all signed the four-power agreement on Berlin; they have also all signed the Helsinki Agreement. But no one can question the fact that it was the United States – among these three powers – which mattered most. Kennedy, his predecessors and his successors, have pledged the support of the United States to the lives and liberty of two million free citizens who live in their Central European lighthouse.

To their credit the West Berliners, generally speaking, understand their awkward and unnatural situation all too well. In particular they know that their first tasks – diplomatically speaking – are to keep calm and to make themselves unforgettable. So do their protectors. One mistake by Corporal Moore in the Invalidenstrasse on the night the wall went up could have instigated something approaching Armageddon. The West Berliners themselves are familiar with crises. But they take their crises calmly. And they do their best, largely by being resolute and cheerful, to ensure that someone, somewhere in the White House, and someone, somewhere in Whitehall does not forget them. Lieutenant Halvorsen, Corporal Moore, Captain Huston, and Flying Officer Weller can never forget the West Berliners. Nor can the West Berliners forget the people who saved them in 1948. Comradeship in adversity is an immensely powerful bond. But it is not easy to convey to those who were not there at the time the strength and importance of the links which bind West Berlin to the Western world. The strength of these links are evident and seem natural to Halvorsen, to Flying Officer Weller, to Captain Huston, and to Corporal Moore, but, if West Berlin is to live its life in liberty, the West's moral and comradely commitment to the West Berliners must also be accepted and understood by the man in the Oval Office. Otherwise the West Berliners will become hostages instead of lighthouse-keepers.

The Four-Power Agreement
on Berlin

The meticulously-negotiated four-power agreement on the status of West Berlin is couched in the sometimes convoluted language of diplomacy. But it is the West Berliners' international charter and Bill of Rights and, in a way, West Berlin's birth certificate as a community of a new kind.

Signed by the governments of the Soviet Union, Britain, France, and the United States, the agreement begins with a four-point declaration of general principles.

1. The four governments will strive to promote the elimination of tension and prevention of complications in the relevant area.

2. The four governments, taking into account their obligations under the Charter of the United Nations, agree that there shall be no use or threat of force in the area and that disputes shall be settled solely by peaceful means.

3. The four governments will mutually respect their individual and joint rights and responsibilities, which remain unchanged.

4. The four governments agree that, irrespective of the differences in legal views, the situation which has developed in the area, and as it is defined in this agreement as well as in the other agreements referred to in this agreement, shall not be changed unilaterally.

The next section deals with traffic between West Berlin and Western Germany, with the status of West Berlin and its relationship with the Federal Republic, and with communications between West Berlin on the one hand and the German Democratic Republic on the other.

The government of the USSR declares that transit traffic by road, rail, and waterways through the territory of the German Democratic Republic of civilian persons and goods between the western sectors of Berlin and the Federal Republic of Germany will be unimpeded; that such traffic will be facilitated so as to take place in the most simple and expeditious manner; and that it will receive preferential treatment . . .

The governments of the French Republic, the United Kingdom, and the United States of America declare that the ties between the western sectors of Berlin and the Federal Republic of Germany will be maintained and developed, taking into account that these sectors continue not to be a constituent part of the Federal Republic of Germany and not to be governed by it . . .

The government of the USSR declares that communications between the western sectors of Berlin and areas bordering on these sectors and those areas of the German Democratic Republic which do not border on these sectors will be improved. Permanent residents of the western sectors will be able to travel through and visit such areas for compassionate, family, religious, cultural, or commercial reasons, or as tourists, under conditions comparable to those applying to other persons entering these areas. The problems of the small enclaves, including Steinstücken, and of other small areas may be solved by exchange of territory.

The Soviet government made a point of consulting the government of the German Democratic Republic and obtaining its agreement. The three Western powers, for their part, consulted Bonn. Both sides inserted into the four-power agreement passages which, in effect, oblige both German governments to respect it and to respect certain parts of it in particular. The passage which commits the West German government most closely reads as follows:

The governments of the French Republic, the United Kingdom, and the United States of America, with reference to part II(b) of the Quadripartite Agreement of this date, and after consultation with the government of the Federal Republic of Germany, have the honour to inform the government of the USSR that:

1. They declare, in the exercise of their rights and responsibilities, that the ties between the western sectors of Berlin and the Federal Republic of Germany will be maintained and developed, taking into account that these sectors continue not to be a constituent part of the Federal Republic of Germany and not to be governed by it. The provisions of the Basic Law of the Federal Republic of Germany and of the constitution operative in the western sectors of Berlin which contradict the above have been suspended and continue not to be in effect.

2. The Federal President, the Federal Government, the Bundesversammlung (joint session of Parliament), the Bundesrat (Upper House), and the Bundestag (Lower House), including their committees and Fraktionen (parliamentary party groups), as well as other state bodies of the Federal Republic of Germany, will not perform in the western sectors of Berlin constitutional or official acts which contradict the provisions of paragraph (1).

3. The government of the Federal Republic of Germany will be represented in the western sectors of Berlin to the authorities of the three governments and to the Senate by a permanent liaison agency.

The Russians, in turn, committed the East German government to a series of undertakings about communications and the right to visit. It reads:

The government of the USSR, with reference to part II(c) of the Quadripartite Agreement of this date and after consultation and agreement with the government of the German Democratic Republic, has the honour to inform the governments of the French Republic, the United Kingdom, and the United States of America that:

1. Communications between the western sectors of Berlin and areas bordering on these sectors and those areas of the German Democratic Republic which do not border on these sectors will be improved.

2. Permanent residents of the western sectors of Berlin will be able to travel through and visit such areas for compassionate, family, religious, cultural, or commercial reasons, or as tourists, under conditions comparable to those applying to other persons entering these areas. In order to facilitate visits and travel as described above by permanent residents of the western sectors of Berlin, additional crossing points will be opened.

The problems of the small enclaves, including Steinstücken, and of other small areas may be solved by exchange of territory . . .

These two annexes to the four-power agreement repeat almost word for word the agreement between the four powers themselves. They have, however, a separate importance because they commit the two German governments to undertakings towards West Berlin which have the force of law internationally and which are guaranteed by all four outside powers – the Soviet Union, the United States, Britain and France. As international treaties go the four-power agreement on Berlin is as watertight and as rational as they come. West Berlin's status may not be the status which the West Berliners desire or would have liked. But at least it has been defined with as much precision as diplomats can put into words.

Biographical Notes

The Generals

LUCIUS D. CLAY was born in Georgia, USA in 1897. He went to West Point in 1918 and joined the engineers. Until he became General Eisenhower's deputy in 1945, he was chiefly famous for having built the Red River Dam, in Denison, Texas in 1938. He succeeded Eisenhower as Commander-in-Chief of the United States Forces in Europe and as Military Governor of the American zone in 1946. He retired from the army in 1949.

WILLIAM TUNNER was born in New Jersey in 1906 and went to West Point in 1928. He joined the US Army Air-Corps, the predecessor to the United States Air Force. He was widely regarded and admired as the Americans' most expert air transport specialist. Besides organizing the airlift over the Himalayas – the Hump – to China for the support of General Wedemeyer's forces, General Tunner also organized the Berlin airlift, and the immense American airlift to Korea in 1950.

ALBERT COADY WEDEMEYER was born in Nebraska in 1897, went to West Point in 1919 and – later – to the German War Academy in Berlin in 1938. During World War II he served in China, the Philippines, Europe, and while in China fulfilled the difficult assignment of chief of staff to Generalissimo Chiang Kai-shek. At the time of the Berlin crisis he served General Bradley, the Chief of Staff of the US Army, as Deputy Chief of Staff for plans and combat operations.

VASILI DANILOVICH SOKOLOVSKY was born at Kozliki near Byelostok in July 1897, into a peasant family. He was a company commander during the Russian civil war, rising to be chief of staff of a rifle division. He graduated from the Military Academy in 1921 after which he served in Central Asia, returning to the Moscow and Urals military areas in the early 1930s. During World War II he served continuously on the Western fronts. He became deputy Commander-in-Chief and later Commander-in-Chief of the Soviet forces in Germany and Military Governor of the Soviet zone.

BRIAN HUBERT ROBERTSON was born on 22 July 1896, the son of William Robertson later to become Field Marshal Sir William Robertson. He served in World War I, was awarded the DSO, the MC, and was mentioned in despatches. He returned to the British Army during World War II in which he served in the Middle East and Italy, becoming General Alexander's Chief Administrative Officer. Promoted to the rank of General in 1947 he became British Commander-in-Chief in Germany and Military Governor.

The Berliners

WILLY BRANDT was born at Lübeck in 1913. He was illegitimate. He was brought up by his maternal grandfather who was an agricultural labourer and a fervent supporter of the Social Democrats. When seventeen he joined the Youth Movement of the Social Democratic Party and was soon in trouble with the Nazis. In 1934 he had to go into exile in Norway and was later deprived of his German nationality. He became a journalist for Norwegian papers and went to Spain in 1937 as a war correspondent. When the Germans invaded Norway in 1940 he escaped to Sweden where he took part in anti-Nazi organizations. In 1945 he returned to Germany, a Norwegian citizen, as press attaché to the Norwegian military mission. In 1948, the year the blockade began, he resumed German nationality.

Brandt became a member of the Executive of the Berlin Social Democrats in 1948, a member of the Senate in 1950, and governing Mayor in 1957. By then he had also been elected to the Federal Parliament in Bonn. He became Minister for Foreign Affairs and Vice Chancellor in 1966. In 1969 he was elected Chancellor and held office until 1974 when he took upon himself the blame for having on his staff an East German spy called Guillaume and resigned. He was awarded the Nobel Peace Prize in 1971 and remains the Social Democrats' chairman.

FERDINAND FRIEDENSBURG was a lawyer and a mining engineer who came from Silesia. Born in 1886, he went into politics in the Weimar period but stayed in that borderland – which has always existed in Germany – between representative politics and administration. He was Vice-President of the Berlin police from 1927 until 1933 when the Nazis dismissed him. In 1935 they arrested him. For a short time after the war he worked in the Soviet zone at his own trade of mining engineer, but came quickly to West Berlin, was warmly welcomed by the Christian Democrats and, when the hour struck, was the acting Mayor who thought it his duty to stay to the end. He died in March, 1972.

ERNST REUTER, the son of a teacher of navigation, was born in Schleswig-Holstein on 29 July 1889. Like many German students, he moved from one university to another – from Marburg to Munich to Münster – and qualified as a teacher in 1912. The same year he joined the Social Democratic Party and by 1913 was a member of its teaching staff in Berlin. Called up in 1915, Reuter was captured by the Russians in 1916. The Russian communists rescued him from a mine in Tula where he had been sent to work and brought him to Moscow. In 1918 they sent him to organize a German Republic among the Germans living on the Volga, but the German revolution, which began later that year, called him home. By December he was back in Berlin, and a member of the German Communist Party. He was arrested almost at once and not released until late in 1919. He became the party secretary for Berlin and then National Secretary, but left the party in 1921 along with many others because of policy differences.

In 1922 Reuter returned to the Social Democratic Party and was elected a Berlin City Councillor in 1926, afterwards becoming a member of the Transport Committee. In May 1931, he moved to Magdeburg where he was elected Mayor. In July 1932 – on the eve of Hitler's accession to power – he was elected to the Reichstag. He was sacked from his job as Mayor of Magdeburg almost as soon as the Nazis came to power and was soon afterwards arrested. After periods in and out of gaol, he left for London fourteen days before the Gestapo came to arrest him for the third time. The government of Turkey offered him a job as a lecturer in economics, which he took. The Reuters then lived in Ankara until the end of the war, after which they returned to Germany as soon as they could and applied themselves at once to the re-creation of the Social Democratic Party. Ernst Reuter died in September 1953.

LOUISE SCHROEDER was born in Altona, Hamburg in 1887, the tenth child of a building worker. She grew up in poverty and in appalling surroundings and became a secretary of legendary prowess. She also, as soon as she could, joined the Social Democrats. She was one of thirty-seven women delegates to the Social Democrats' first congress after World War I, and was presently elected to the Reichstag. One of the first things Hitler did when he came to power was to make Louise Schroeder report twice daily to the police. Soon after World War II Louise Schroeder refused to join the SED. She was acting Mayor for eighteen months from 5 May 1947 in the place of Ernst Reuter. She saw it as her main task to make the winter of 1947–8 less horrible for the people of Berlin than the preceding winter had been. She died in June 1957.

OTTO SUHR was born into the middle class at Oldenburg on the North German plain on 17 August 1894. He attended high school in Leipzig and, after one term at Leipzig University, was called up by the army and began his political education. He learned from his Silesian comrades the realities of working-class life in Germany before World War I. Lieutenant Suhr, who distinguished himself in the field, became a Social Democrat there and then. After the war Suhr returned to Leipzig University. He plunged into student politics but felt the need to keep close to the workers. He moved to Kassel as a party official to build up the movement, he strengthened his links and the party's with the trade unions and lectured in colleges of further education up and down the country, teaching politics and socialism and trade union policy. Eventually he came to Berlin. His last great meeting there was broken up by the police and after Hitler's take-over he was not allowed to speak again until 4 July 1945, after the Allies had captured Germany. He died in August 1957.

Sources

Among the many sources of information about Berlin's post-war history the most important are the papers of the US State Department and of the British Foreign Office and also the exchanges between General Clay and the American Secretary for the Army, Royall. In the matter of the blockade and the airlift, the Air History Division of the US Department of Defense and the Air History Branch of the British Ministry of Defence offer valuable material to the student of this time. The comprehensive files kept by General William H. Tunner of the United States Air Force also illuminate the story brightly, as they do the stories of his other major undertakings in India, Vietnam and Korea.

Among the many books published about Berlin there are:

Decision in Germany, Lucius D. Clay, London, 1950.

Over the Hump, William H. Tunner, New York, 1964.

The End of the Third Reich, Vasili I. Chuikov, London, 1967.

Luftbrücke, Berlin, Klaus Scherff, Stuttgart, 1976.

The Balance of Power, Helmut Schmidt, London, 1971.

Meeting at Potsdam, Charles L. Mee, London, 1975.

Index

Index